SpringerBriefs in Public Health

For further volumes:
http://www.springer.com/series/10138

Troy Tassier

The Economics
of Epidemiology

 Springer

Troy Tassier
Department of Economics
Fordham University
New York
USA

ISSN 2192-3698 ISSN 2192-3701 (electronic)
ISBN 978-3-642-38119-5 ISBN 978-3-642-38120-1 (eBook)
DOI 10.1007/978-3-642-38120-1
Springer Heidelberg New York Dordrecht London

Library of Congress Control Number: 2013941342

© The Author(s) 2013
This work is subject to copyright. All rights are reserved by the Publisher, whether the whole or part of the material is concerned, specifically the rights of translation, reprinting, reuse of illustrations, recitation, broadcasting, reproduction on microfilms or in any other physical way, and transmission or information storage and retrieval, electronic adaptation, computer software, or by similar or dissimilar methodology now known or hereafter developed. Exempted from this legal reservation are brief excerpts in connection with reviews or scholarly analysis or material supplied specifically for the purpose of being entered and executed on a computer system, for exclusive use by the purchaser of the work. Duplication of this publication or parts thereof is permitted only under the provisions of the Copyright Law of the Publisher's location, in its current version, and permission for use must always be obtained from Springer. Permissions for use may be obtained through RightsLink at the Copyright Clearance Center. Violations are liable to prosecution under the respective Copyright Law.
The use of general descriptive names, registered names, trademarks, service marks, etc. in this publication does not imply, even in the absence of a specific statement, that such names are exempt from the relevant protective laws and regulations and therefore free for general use.
While the advice and information in this book are believed to be true and accurate at the date of publication, neither the authors nor the editors nor the publisher can accept any legal responsibility for any errors or omissions that may be made. The publisher makes no warranty, express or implied, with respect to the material contained herein.

Printed on acid-free paper

Springer is part of Springer Science+Business Media (www.springer.com)

Preface

The spread of an infectious disease is a social as well as a biological process. An infectious disease spreads as a function of its and our biology but it is also aided by a host of social factors from the face to face interactions of people to the decisions people make regarding vaccines and hand hygiene. In this book I give a brief introduction to epidemiology from the perspective of one of the social sciences, economics.

Fundamental to the study of economics are the choices that people make. People choose whether to spend their money on ice cream, new shoes, or to save. Of course one cannot spend money that he does not have either from past earnings, savings, or borrowing. Thus economists study the choices people make in conjunction with the constraints they face. I have $100, what do I do with it? The choices that economists study are not solely monetary decisions. In our day to day lives we also choose whether to go to a party or stay home, whether we take public transportation or drive to work, and whether to get a yearly influenza vaccine or not. Each of these decisions is also a constrained choice that depends on things like whether our friends invite us to a party, whether we have enough money to buy a car, and whether we have enough time to be vaccinated. All of these decisions can have an impact on the spread of an infectious disease both from an individual perspective and a population level perspective. If we go to a party, or take public transportation we expose ourselves to the risk of acquiring an infectious disease. In addition, if we become infected we also make it more likely that other people in the population become infected. If I catch a cold at a party on Saturday night, I expose my coworkers to the virus on Monday morning. Economists call this type of interdependence an externality. My choice (in this case to go to a party) has an effect on other people who do not take part in my choice. Similarly, decisions like getting a yearly influenza vaccine not only protect me, but also partly protect the people I come in contact with because I cannot infect them (assuming the vaccine is effective). Further some of the choices we make and the consequences of those choices depend on the people with whom we interact. If everyone around me makes risky decisions with regard to infectious disease that may influence how careful I am. Thus we live in an interconnected web of individual decisions, incentives, and risks. These are exactly the topics that economists study. In this book I use economic modeling to attempt to better understand and describe how infectious disease spreads and the choices that individuals and policy makers choose in response.

In this book I will provide a basic introduction to the ways in which economics can be applied to a set of basic epidemiological phenomena. The goal of the book is to provide a starting point for a discussion between three groups of people interested in the spread of infectious disease: medical professionals, social scientists, and public health officials (as well as students pursuing careers in these fields). In doing so I provide a basic introduction to some elements of each of these fields so that this discussion has a starting point. Hopefully, if I have done my job well, economists will learn some basic epidemiology, and public health and medical professionals will learn a little economics that can be applied to their field.

As an outline, I begin by discussing the basic structure of the most simple models of epidemiology and introduce readers with a social science background to some of the core concepts of epidemiology. With this starting point, I use these core concepts to discuss how the spread of an infectious disease creates economic externalities. Further, this externalities perspective allows me to discuss how an economist would view public health interventions to stop or slow the spread of an epidemic. The next sections of the book introduce both reality and complications into our understanding of epidemics. As mentioned above, many infectious diseases that interest us today spread from person to person. This makes an understanding of the structure of interactions between people paramount in understanding the spread of an infectious disease. Thus, I provide an introduction to the field of social network analysis and discuss how to use measures common to this field to better understand the spread of an epidemic. Finally, again as an economist, I must reintroduce the element of choice and more explicitly strategic choice into the discussion. We not only make decisions for various personal reasons, we also make decisions in conjunction with others. For instance, policy makers attempt to induce individuals to make decisions that benefit society, for example, the provision of a subsidy for a vaccine. We also make choices individually that have effects on each other's well being. For instance if your closest friend chooses to be vaccinated for a particular infectious disease, your incentive to be vaccinated diminishes because there is one less person you know that can infect you. Both of these examples suggest that there can be strategic elements to public and individual health decisions. As such I provide a brief discussion of game theory in the final section of the book.

I would like to acknowledge several sources that allowed me to write this book. My interest in the intersection of infectious disease and economics has two origins. The first is a group of colleagues who sparked my interest in the field through their own work while I was a post-doctoral research fellow at the University of Michigan Center for the Study of Complex Systems. Most notably, Mark Newman, Carl Simon, and Chris Warren all had interests at the intersection of social networks, economics, and epidemiology that inspired and educated me. My advisor, Scott Page gave me the freedom to investigate a diverse set of topics as well as providing unending sources of encouragement and guidance. The second origin was Phil Polgreen and Alberto Segre who brought me into the fold of the

Computational Epidemiology Research Group at the University of Iowa and gave me access to very rich sources of data. More recently, each fall for the past decade, Henry Schwalbenberg has allowed me to teach the course from which this book developed in the Fordham University International Political Economy and Development program to classes of exceptional students. Fordham University, both my home economics department and the university in general, has been very supportive of my research agenda and generously provided a research fellowship that gave me the opportunity to complete this manuscript. I am grateful to Barbara Fess at Springer for supporting and encouraging this project. Finally, much gratitude and love to Mary Beth, Katherine, and Nicholas for your love, support, and never-ending moments of joy and happiness.

Contents

Part I Epidemic Modeling

1 An Introduction to Epidemic Modeling.................... 3
   1.1 Categorical Models 4

2 Simple Epidemics and SIS Models 9
   2.1 Introduction 9
   2.2 The First Model: A Simple Epidemic 9
   2.3 A Full SIS Model 12
   2.4 Steady State 14
   2.5 Computational Implementation 15

3 SIR 17
   3.1 Introduction 17
   3.2 The SIR Model 17
       3.2.1 Dynamics................................... 18
   3.3 Epidemic Threshold and Steady States................ 19
   3.4 Computational Analysis 20
   3.5 Herd Immunity 23
   3.6 Non-Constant Populations............................ 24

Part II Merging Economics and Epidemiology

4 Economic Modeling and Epidemiology 31
   4.1 Economic Utility.................................... 31
   4.2 Utility and Epidemic Modeling....................... 32
   4.3 The Economics of Prevention 33
       4.3.1 Individual Prevention Decisions 34
       4.3.2 Public Prevention Decisions................. 34
       4.3.3 Costs and Benefits of Public Health Decisions 37
   Reference... 39

5	**Econometrics and Epidemiology**...........................	41

Part III An Introduction to Social Interactions

6	**Interaction Networks: An Introduction**....................	47
	6.1 Network Properties	49
	6.2 Characteristic Path Length	50
	6.3 Clustering...	53
	6.4 Centrality	55
	6.4.1 Measuring Centrality............................	58
	6.5 Degree Distribution	59
	6.5.1 Who Has More Friends?	61
	6.6 Dynamic Networks	63
	References	65

Part IV Strategic Decision Making

7	**Strategic Public Health Interventions**.....................	69
	7.1 Purposeful Behavior....................................	70
	7.1.1 Varying Risk	70
	7.1.2 Varying Risk Tolerance..........................	72
	7.1.3 Targeted Intervention	75
	References	77
8	**Strategic Individual Decision Making**.....................	79
	8.1 A Brief Introduction to Game Theory	79
	8.1.1 Classes of 2×2 Games........................	81
	8.2 A Vaccination Game	84
	8.3 Peer Effects	89
9	**Conclusion**..	93
	Reference..	94

Part I
Epidemic Modeling

Part 1

Chapter 1
An Introduction to Epidemic Modeling

To begin, I discuss the basic ideas behind the theoretical modeling of epidemics. Briefly, in constructing a model of the spread of an infectious disease we first identify a set of categories or states that individuals may be in that are important in describing the course of an epidemic. For instance individuals may be infected with a given disease, they may be susceptible to acquiring it, or they may be vaccinated and protected against acquiring it. Once the categories are identified we then group individuals in our population of interest into these categories according to their status. The important dynamics of the course of an epidemic occur because of transitions individuals make between these states. Individuals may go from being susceptible to being infected (and infecting others) to being recovered. Or they may go from being susceptible, to receiving a vaccination, to being immune from becoming infected. The description of an epidemic states how these transitions between categories occur across time and answers how many individuals are in a given category at each point in time? To do this within a model we need to calculate the rates at which these various transitions occur (infection, recovery, death, etc.) Initially I describe these transition rates between states abstractly with generic parameters, like α and κ. When one moves to empirical consideration one can use statistics to estimate these transition rates or use underlying knowledge of biology to fix values to these transition rates. As these transitions occur individuals move between categories and thereby change the population sizes in each of these categories. Once this modeling process is specified one can write down a set of equations as a formal description of the model. The equations can then be used to describe the system outcomes either analytically, statistically, or computationally.

Before I venture too far I want to point out that all models have some details that are inaccurate. For instance, each individual in a population has a slightly different immune system that may make them more or less likely to acquire a particular infectious disease. The point of a model is not to state every detail precisely but to help us sort out the logical consequences of ideas and assumptions. Models should not be judged based on the level of detail and parsimony that they contain but instead on how accurately they allow us to answer questions of interest. One model may be superior to another in one context and inferior to the same model in another. The context depends on the questions that we are interested in pursuing. As an example consider two model cars. One model has intricate details of all of the interior components of the car. Another has no *inside* at all; it is simply a mock-up of the body of the car. The first model would be excellent for testing the ergonomics of the car; the second would be excellent for testing aerodynamics. The types of questions that you are interested in answering determine the style of models that you want to build. In this book we will work to build simple models that describe fundamental properties of epidemics that can be used in conjunction with economic analysis. I also will describe how these fundamental models can be refined to include more details that may be necessary to perform empirical investigations at a more detailed level in various populations. I now begin to discuss this initial model building process.

1.1 Categorical Models

When I construct a model for a particular system, I first make a categorical model or what is sometimes called a "box model" so-called because it divides the host population up into boxes according to epidemiological status. The most common categories are:

- Susceptible: These are hosts (usually individuals in our interest for this book) that are susceptible to infection.
- Infected: These are hosts that have been infected by an infectious disease of interest.
- Infective: These are hosts that are infected, and capable of infecting other hosts. Note that some infected hosts may not be infective. Sometimes individuals are infected but have no ability to pass on the infection. This sometimes occurs when a host is initially infected but the infection has not developed enough within the host to be passed on to others yet. It also is possible that some individuals will be asymptomatic. They are infected and infective but unaware of their state because they have no symptoms.

The three states above exist in any model of an epidemic. In addition, we might have categories such as:

- Recovered (or Removed): These are hosts that have acquired immunity to the disease, or been quarantined, or vaccinated, or otherwise been made unavailable for infection. This may also include individuals that have died and thereby been removed from the population of interest.
- Exposed (or Latent): These are hosts that have been infected but are incubating the disease; they are infected but not yet infective.

I refer to the number of individuals in these categories as the state variables of our system. The list of categories or states we have in a particular model depends on the biology of a particular disease: Is there an incubation period? Do any hosts

1.1 Categorical Models

recover? If so, once recovered, do they acquire immunity or do they become susceptible again?

I can write down a categorical model in the form of a picture, for example:

$$S \to I \to R$$

or,

$$S \leftrightarrow I$$

In the first example individuals in category susceptible (S) can transition to infected (I) and then to recovered (R). Once individuals pass through the infected category they do not return tot the susceptible category and cannot be infected again. In the second example individuals can go from S to I and back to S. Individuals that recover from being infected return to the susceptible category where they can once again be infected.

Following convention, I refer to these models by their acronyms. Some common examples are:

- SI (also known as the "simple epidemic") is an epidemic where hosts never recover,
- SIS one where they recover but become susceptible again (e.g. gonorrhea),
- SIR where they recover and gain immunity (e.g. measles, influenza),
- SEIR where there is an incubation period, etc...

Sometimes, one given disease may be modeled using different categories. For instance HIV is most appropriately an SIR type infectious disease. Individuals are susceptible, pass into the infected category and remain there until death (either from AIDS or other causes). But, given the longevity of the infected period it is sometimes modeled as an SI disease especially when the time interval of interest is short (maybe one year) relative to the number of years an individual lives with HIV (which may be decades).

Next one considers the transitions between various categories: how do individuals move from one category to another? Here are some examples:

- birth (entering the S category from outside the current population, or possibly entering I if there is vertical transmission where some individuals are born infected),
- migration (like birth this could occur as flows into any of the states above depending on the characteristics of the disease),
- "natural" (non-disease-related) death (this could happen in any category),
- disease-induced mortality (leaving I as the result of a death event associated with the individual being in state I),
- infection (moving from S to I—usually as a result of contact with another host),
- recovery (moving from I to R).

The resulting model might look like this:

$$\overrightarrow{birth}\ S\ \overrightarrow{infection}\ I\ \overrightarrow{recovery, death}\ R$$

Next I need to quantify the transitions: how fast do individuals get infected, die, and how do these transition rates depend on the numbers or densities of hosts in different categories? To keep track of the number of individuals in each category I adopt the convention that an upper case letter identifies the number of individuals in each state. For examples, I can consider a simple epidemic model of the *SI* form. S will be the number of susceptible individuals in the population, I will be the number of infective individuals. As an example, the following is one set of assumptions:

- birth may occur at a constant per capita rate and may come from just the susceptible population or births may come from both susceptible and infective hosts. In the latter case, the number of new individuals born is the birth rate b multiplied by the sum of number of susceptible and infective individuals in the population, $b(S+I)$;
- natural death at rate d occurs at a constant per capita rate in each category: dS, dI;
- disease-induced mortality occurs at a constant per capita rate: aI;
- infection is often assumed to be proportional to both S and I. This assumption implies that we treat individuals as though they are gas molecules, which often is not a bad first approximation. If we double the number of susceptibles or the number of infectives, we double the overall infection rate (do both and we quadruple it): $g(S/N)I$. So, in this case, think of there being I infective individuals in the population. If an infective individual comes into contact with a susceptible individual the susceptible individual becomes infected. If each infective individual contacts g other individuals some of them will be susceptible and some will be already infected. If I assume that infected individuals cannot be more infected than they already are, the only contacts that result in a transition are when an infective individual comes in contact with a susceptible individual. So, I need to normalize the g number of contacts by the fraction of category S individuals in the population, which is S/N, where N is the total number of individuals in the population.

Because the spread of a disease is a dynamic process I want to keep track of the state variables over time. Thus I denote the time period by the subscript t on each of our state variables. For example, the variable S_t indicates the number of susceptible individuals in time period t.

With these assumptions I can write a set of equations describing the model as follows:

$$S_{t+1} = S_t + b(S_t + I_t) - dS_t - g(S_t/N_t)I_t \qquad (1.1)$$

$$I_{t+1} = I_t + g(S_t/N_t)I_t - dI_t - aI_t \qquad (1.2)$$

1.1 Categorical Models

For those familiar with econometrics or statistics these equations can be written in a form that one can use to estimate the model parameters using ordinary least squares (OLS):

$$S_{t+1} = (1 + b - d)S_t + bI_t - g(S_t/N_t)I_t \tag{1.3}$$

$$I_{t+1} = (1 - d - a)I_t + g(S_t/N_t)I_t \tag{1.4}$$

Given a set of time series data on infections and the population size, you can get estimates for each parameter of the model by running a regression of the following form:

$$S_{t+1} = \beta_1 S_t + \beta_2 I_t - \beta_3 I_t S_t / N_t \tag{1.5}$$

$$I_{t+1} = \beta_4 I_t + \beta_5 I_t S_t / N_t \tag{1.6}$$

You get the estimate for b directly from the coefficient on I_t when you estimate Eq. 1.3. Once you have b you can then calculate d from the coefficient on S_t in the same equation. Once you have d, you can calculate a from the coefficient on I_t in Eq. 1.4. Because you know N_t (as the sum of S_t and I_t) you can calculate g from the coefficient on the interaction term $I_t S_t$ in either equation. Thus this model will allow you to estimate all of the important parameters of interest for the spread of this epidemic.

With these preliminary ideas introduced we will proceed to discuss additional models and the properties and characteristics of each.

Chapter 2
Simple Epidemics and SIS Models

2.1 Introduction

Next I analyze some formal models of epidemics. In all of these initial models I make some simplifying assumptions that will aid with the introductory analysis. Later in the chapter and in subsequent chapters I will generalize the models to make them more realistic. Further by the end of these introductory sections you will be prepared to make additional assumptions and generalizations on your own in exactly the same framework introduced here. However I want to point out that making simplifying assumptions in these early chapters, does not make these models invalid or of no use. Often times simple models can reveal a great deal about the dynamics of interest in the spread of an epidemic. Further the solution concepts that I use in these simple introductory models will also apply to more complicated models.

I have two goals in this chapter: One is to introduce the reader to an SI model or what is sometimes called a simple epidemic. I will use this model to introduce the concept of an epidemic threshold, the level at which an epidemic will "take off" and grow in a population. Second, I will introduce the general SIS model framework and discuss the concept of the reproduction number and an epidemic steady state.

2.2 The First Model: A Simple Epidemic

To begin I start with the simplest possible dynamic model of an epidemic, an SI model. I want to monitor the number of individuals in the population who are infected with the disease of interest. Again I will use the variable t to denote the time period. I use N_t to denote the total size of the population in period t. In this first model, I have two categories, those that are susceptible to being infected by the disease, denoted by S, and those that are infected (and infective), denoted by I. I label the number of those infected in period t as I_t and the number susceptible in period t as S_t. where $I_t + S_t = N_t$. Individuals go from being susceptible to a disease to being infected and once infected, they never recover and remain in the population forever. Thus the progression of the disease from the standpoint of an individual is susceptible–infected or SI.

Assume that $N_t = N$ for all t. In other words there is a constant population size. Further assume that all the people in the population are the same people from period to period. Note that these are two different assumptions. One example where N_t is constant but with turnover in the population would be if there were equal birth and death rates in the population. In this example, the population size would be constant but some of the people in the population would be different each period. For now I ignore this and assume that there is a constant unchanging population.

Individuals potentially move from the susceptible to the infected group when a susceptible person comes in contact with an infected person. What counts as a contact varies with the disease. Sometimes diseases are transmitted through sexual contact or are carried in blood as in HIV. In other cases one only needs to be near a person as the disease is carried via the air we breath as in SARS or influenza. In addition even if you come in contact with someone it is not always guaranteed that the disease will be transmitted. For instance only a small fraction of sexual contacts between an infective and a susceptible person result in the transmission of HIV. I denote the probability of a contact between a susceptible and an infected person resulting in transmission of the infectious disease to be α.

Suppose there are I_0 infected individuals in the initial period of the model. In epidemics we are interested in how the disease will spread. Thus what we really want to know in many cases is how many infected individuals there will be in the next period. In other words we want to know I_1, and then I_2 and then .... We want to know how the spread of the disease will progress.

I begin by looking at the transition from period 0 to period 1. In period 0 there are I_0 infected individuals. Call this the state of the system at time 0. New individuals get infected by coming in contact with members of the infected population. Assume that each infected person contacts γ non-infected people in each period. Thus the number of possible new infections is γI_0. But not all of the contacts result in an infection. As stated above, suppose that only α percent of contacts result in an infection. Thus each infected individual results in $\gamma \alpha$ new infections in the subsequent period. Now write out an equation that describes this process:

$$I_1 = I_0 + \gamma \alpha I_0 = (1 + \gamma \alpha) I_0 \qquad (2.1)$$

Now write the equation for period 2:

$$I_2 = I_1 + \gamma \alpha I_1 \qquad (2.2)$$

This is the same equation but with different time subscripts. Now substitute Eq. 2.1 into Eq. 2.2 to get:

$$I_2 = (1 + \gamma \alpha) I_0 + \gamma \alpha ((1 + \gamma \alpha) I_0) = (1 + \gamma \alpha)^2 I_0 \qquad (2.3)$$

2.2 The First Model: A Simple Epidemic

Similarly, write the following for I_3 and onward. In general the following equation describes the general solution of the model:

$$I_t = (1 + \gamma\alpha)^t I_0 \tag{2.4}$$

The number of people currently infected in period t is 1 plus the product of the contact and transmission parameters raised to the power t multiplied by the initial size of the infected population.

Note that the epidemic will always grow until the entire population is infected as long as both $\gamma > 0$ and $\alpha > 0$. In the simple SI model the only long run outcome is for all individuals in the population to become infected.

Now, change the model slightly. In the previous model once an individual was infected she remained there forever. The only transition in the model was from category S to category I. Now, instead, assume that once infected each individual in the population returns to the susceptible population after one time period. This is a new modeling transition, where agents can go from susceptible to infected and back to susceptible again. With this new assumption the basic equation describing out model becomes:

$$I_{t+1} = I_t + \gamma\alpha I_t - I_t = \gamma\alpha I_t \tag{2.5}$$

Again, trace through the beginning of an epidemic by starting with period 1 and finding I_1:

$$I_1 = I_0 + \gamma\alpha I_0 - I_0 = \gamma\alpha I_0 \tag{2.6}$$

Again, iterating forward leads to:

$$I_2 = \gamma\alpha I_1 = (\gamma\alpha)^2 I_0 \tag{2.7}$$

Or, more generally:

$$I_{t+1} = (\gamma\alpha)^t I_0 \tag{2.8}$$

This equation has more interesting possibilities. Let us analyze how this system will behave by looking at the number of infected persons in period t where t is far into the future. In other words t is large, say 1,000. Suppose that there is one infected person in the initial period and that γ is 5 and α is 0.1. Will there be many people infected or a few at period 1,000? Note that $\alpha\gamma = 0.5$. So we expect that there will be 0.5^{1000} people infected in period 1,000. You can check on your calculators if you like but this is a VERY small number, essentially 0. What if we increase α to 0.3? Now we get 1.5^{1000}, a VERY big number! What happens if α is 0.2? We get $1^{1000} = 1$. Lets try one more, let I_0 be 1,000,000 and α be 0.19. Thus in period 1,000 we would have $(0.19 * 5)^{1000} * 1,000,000 = 0.95^{1000} * 1,000,000$ which again is essentially 0.

What you have probably already noticed is that if $\alpha\gamma < 1$ the number of infected individuals decreases to 0 very rapidly; the disease disappears. If $\alpha\gamma > 1$ the number of infected individuals keeps increasing; the disease spreads throughout the population. This is sometimes called the *epidemic threshold*. Now what does this really mean? How can we interpret this result? If the number of contacts multiplied by the transmission rate is less than one this means that each infected person infects less than one person on average. So, the number of infected individuals will decrease. It is like the reproduction and population models you may have studied in biology class, if each person has less than one offspring the population will die out. But if the average number of offspring is greater than one the population will grow. Just like our model when the average number of people infected is greater than one; the disease continues to spread to a larger and larger fraction of the population. Thus we reach the epidemic threshold whenever greater than one person is infected by each infected person.

The model of this section has some weaknesses that we will correct in the next section. But the main point of the model is that we can understand most of what is going on if we look at just a couple parameters in the model. And, from a public policy standpoint if we can alter those parameters we can control an epidemic. As an example, if we can limit the number of contacts of infected people with non-infected people so that we are below the epidemic threshold we can end the epidemic. Further, it may not take a large action to break free of an epidemic if we are near the epidemic threshold. Suppose that each infected individual in a population has 11 contacts with susceptible individuals and the transmission rate is 0.10. We would be above the epidemic threshold and the epidemic would grow very quickly. After 100 time periods there would be nearly 14,000 individuals infected. But, if we could decrease the number of contacts by just 1, to 10, the epidemic would stabilize. And, if we were able to decrease the number of contacts to 9 the epidemic would die out quickly as well. (If we decreased the contacts to 9 at period 100 it would take less than 50 periods for the number of infected individuals to drop to less than 100 and by period 190 there would be less than one individual infected on average.) The lesson here is that sometimes even large epidemics can be precariously balanced at the edge of eradication. On the other hand, sometimes it can take only a small nudge to turn a small public health issue into a very large one.

2.3 A Full SIS Model

I kept the model of the last section overly simplistic in order to introduce some key ideas. First, I used difference equations to study a diffusion process. And second, I introduced some key parameters that will be used throughout the book. In this section I more fully develop the SIS model to a form that one is likely to encounter in policy and research discussions of diseases that fit the SIS framework.

First, in the final model of the last section I assumed that each contact of an infected individual was with a non-infected, or susceptible, individual. It is more realistic to assume that the number of susceptible contacts is a function of the

2.3 A Full SIS Model

number of susceptible persons in the population. Second, I assumed that each infected person was fully recovered after one time period. This may be true if I am measuring time in weeks or months, but it probably isn't true for some diseases if I am measuring time in days or shorter intervals. Thus I would like the model to allow for the possibility that it takes multiple time periods for someone to move from the infected group back to the susceptible group.

I can do this in the following way. First define two new state variables that will measure the percentage of the total population that are susceptible and infected. Let $i_t = I_t/N_t$ be the percent of the population that is currently infected. Define $s_t = S_t/N_t$ as the percent of the population that is currently susceptible. I also define a new parameter κ that measures the percent of the population that recovers from a disease each period. Thus if the time to recover is 3 time periods then $\kappa = 1/3$. This means that one-third of the population should recover each period on average.[1]

I am now ready to write a system of equations that will describe the full SIS model of epidemics:

$$I_{t+1} = I_t - \kappa I_t + \alpha \gamma s_t I_t \tag{2.9}$$

$$S_{t+1} = S_t + \kappa I_t - \alpha \gamma s_t I_t \tag{2.10}$$

In these equations κI_t individuals recover each period and thus leave the infected group and re-enter the susceptible group and $\alpha \gamma s_t I_t$ individuals enter the infected group and leave the susceptible group. Notice that the change in the infected group always equals the change in the susceptible group when there is a constant population. Thus $S_t + I_t = S_{t+1} + I_{t+1} = N$ if the population is constant.

Equivalently write these equations using the proportion state variables:

$$i_{t+1} = i_t - \kappa i_t + \alpha \gamma s_t i_t \tag{2.11}$$

$$s_{t+1} = s_t + \kappa i_t - \alpha \gamma s_t i_t \tag{2.12}$$

Now, with these equations written, use them to understand the epidemic threshold in the SIS model. First ask the question: when will the number of infected individuals be increasing? Intuitively we can reason through this process by just looking at the equations. If more people flow into the infective state than flow out this means that the level of infective individuals is increasing. If the opposite is true (more flow out than in) the level of infective individuals is decreasing. Thus the epidemic threshold is determined by whether $\kappa i_t > \alpha \gamma s_t i_t$ or $\kappa i_t < \alpha \gamma s_t i_t$.

If $\kappa > \alpha \gamma s_t$ this means that more individuals leave the infective state than enter it. Thus the level of the disease is decreasing. If $\kappa < \alpha \gamma s_t$ this means that more

---

[1] It may seem that this is a weird assumption since it may be that there are different numbers of people infected in each period. Thus different numbers of people should recover each period. I will show in a moment that if the model reaches steady state this assumption will be valid.

individuals enter the infective state than leave it. Thus the level of the disease is increasing. Another way to write this inequality is: $\frac{\alpha \gamma s_t}{\kappa}$. This is the epidemic threshold for the SIS model. If this fraction is greater than one the level of infective individuals increases (more than one susceptible individual is infected by each infective individual). If it is less than one the level of infective individuals decreases (fewer than one susceptible individual is infected by each infective individual.)

Closely related to the epidemic threshold is the concept of the *reproduction number*. By the analysis above, note that each infected individual is expected to reproduce $\frac{\alpha \gamma s_t}{\kappa}$ new infections in the population. This number is critical in the beginning of an epidemic. If the reproduction number is not above one then an epidemic never occurs. Further, because we are often interested in this number at the beginning of an epidemic, we are often interested in this value when most of the population is susceptible, in other words when s_t is near one. In this case $\frac{\alpha \gamma s_t}{\kappa} \approx \frac{\alpha \gamma}{\kappa}$. Epidemiologists refer to this number as the reproduction number in the population and following convention I write it as $R_0 = \frac{\alpha \gamma}{\kappa}$.

If we move away from the initial period of an epidemic, we notice that one thing different about this model compared to our previous one is that one of our state variables enters the equation for the epidemic threshold, s_t. If $\frac{\alpha \gamma s_t}{\kappa} > 1$ the disease spreads and the number of susceptible individuals decreases. Thus the fraction gets smaller in the next period. If $\frac{\alpha \gamma s_t}{\kappa} < 1$ the disease begins to die out and the number of susceptible individuals increases. Thus the fraction gets bigger in the next period. For those of you who have taken economics courses this reasoning may sound familiar. It may sound like a process that is working its way toward an equilibrium. In fact, that is exactly what we will see in many cases here. The lack of susceptible individuals slows the epidemic when there are many infective individuals; and many susceptible individuals increases the spread of the epidemic when there are few infective individuals. The number of available hosts (or susceptible individuals) introduces negative feedback into the SIS model.

What would be the case where the disease reaches equilibrium? By this I mean the number of susceptibles and infectives is in steady state; both are constant proportions of the population. This would be the case if $\frac{\alpha \gamma s_t}{\kappa} = 1$ or, rearranging, $s_t = \frac{\kappa}{\alpha \gamma}$. This would define a steady state of the system where s_t and i_t are constant in all periods moving forward in time.

2.4 Steady State

The first full model of epidemics can be analyzed a little more formally by looking at the steady state of our system of equations. Again, for those of you who have taken previous economics courses you may think of a steady state as an equilibrium: a situation where a system is not changing. In this model think of a steady state as a condition or set of conditions where our state variables, I_t and S_t, do not

2.4 Steady State

change from period to period; they are constant. To find the steady state, find a solution to the system of equations above where $S_t = S_{t+1}$ and $I_t = I_{t+1}$. One way to do this is to drop the time subscript on our equations above and solve for s and i. Thus look for a solution to the following set of equations:

$$i = i - \kappa i + \alpha \gamma s i \tag{2.13}$$

$$s = s + \kappa i - \alpha \gamma s i \tag{2.14}$$

To solve these equations first rewrite Eq. 2.13 as:

$$\kappa i = \alpha \gamma s i \tag{2.15}$$

which can then be written as:

$$\bar{s} = \frac{\kappa}{\alpha \gamma} \tag{2.16}$$

This is the steady state value of the proportion of the population that is susceptible. It is the same equation as we found above from our intuitive understanding of the epidemic. Further, because we know that $s_t + i_t = 1$, we know that the steady state value of the infected proportion of the population is $i_t = 1 - s_t$ or:

$$\bar{i} = 1 - \frac{\kappa}{\alpha \gamma} \tag{2.17}$$

Note the intuitive properties of the comparative statics of these equations. As the number of contacts of an infected person or the transmission probability increases the number of susceptible individuals decreases (and the number of infected individuals increases). As the time to recover increases (meaning κ decreases) the number of susceptible individuals decreases (the number of infected people increases.)

Next we will cover some simple examples to view how parameter changes affect these outcomes and to check our analytical predictions of steady state values of susceptible and infective individuals in the population.

2.5 Computational Implementation

One of the advantages of using simple models and difference equations (instead of differential equations) for introducing these topics is the ease of incorporating the model into a simple spreadsheet program like Excel. One can simply input the set of equations above into the spreadsheet, plug in some parameters of interest, and view the outcome of the models. In this subsection I present some graphs displaying these outcomes. To start note that the only time that α and γ appear in the equations above is as the product $\alpha \gamma$. To simplify notation combine these two parameters into one parameter β. To start suppose that $\kappa = 0.5$ and $\beta = 0.8$. This

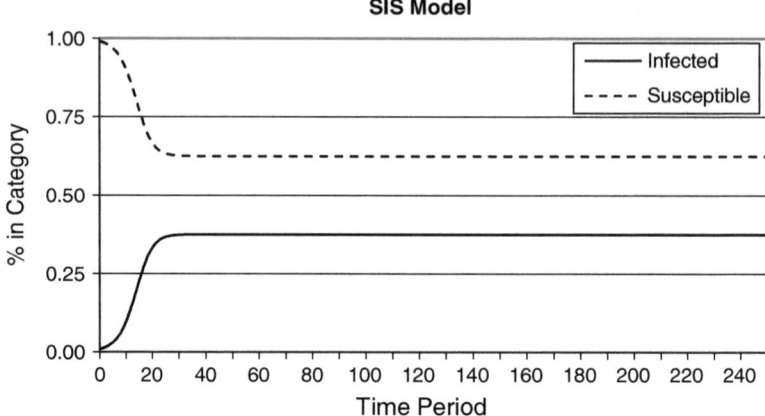

Fig. 2.1 Simple SIS model with $\beta = 0.8$ and $\kappa = 0.5$

means that each infected person recovers in two time periods on average (again you may think of a time period as perhaps a day) and each infected person potentially contacts and infects an average of 0.8 persons per time period. We also need to specify an initial fraction of the infected population. Because an epidemic usually begins with a small set of infected individuals, let us choose this value to be $i_0 = 0.01$.

In Fig. 2.1 you see that the fraction of infected individuals in the population increases quickly up to 37.5 % of the population. This is exactly the steady state level that we expect, $1 - \frac{\kappa}{\beta} = 1 - \frac{0.5}{0.8} = 3/8$ infected individuals. Also note that this level does not depend on the fraction of infective individuals in period 0. The steady state is determined only by the infection and recovery parameters of the model.

Now let us see how the parameters affect the steady state level. To start, increase the recovery rate of the model, κ, to 0.6, for example, and the steady fraction of infected individuals drops to 1/4 of the population. Increase κ further to 0.7 the steady state fraction drops further. Increase the level of κ far enough, we go below the epidemic threshold and the steady state level of infective individuals drops to 0; the disease disappears. This happens exactly where the ratio $\frac{\kappa}{\beta} = 1$ or when $\kappa \geq \beta$. Thus, the steady states of the model depend only on the ratio of β and κ.

Similarly one can increase or decrease the size of the steady state fraction of infective individuals by changing β. If I return to the $\kappa = 0.5$ and increase β to 1.0 I increase the steady state level of infective individuals in the population to 50 %. Or if I decrease β to a level of 0.5 or less I pass below the epidemic threshold and the epidemic disappears.

The SIS model is simple in the sense that one of two things happens, either the system is above the epidemic threshold, converges to a steady state and stays there, or the system is below the epidemic threshold, and the system remains at a steady state with no infective individuals in the population. As we will see in the next chapter, SIR models can have more complicated behavior.

Chapter 3
SIR

3.1 Introduction

In the last chapter I discussed a model of disease spread where individuals were susceptible to a disease, potentially infected with the disease, and then recover to once again become susceptible. This was the standard SIS model. In this chapter I study a different model of infectious disease. This model is appropriate for infectious diseases in which the individual contracting the disease becomes immune to future infections after recovery. This model is called SIR for Susceptible–Infected–Recovered. As a variant on this title SIR can also stand for Susceptible–Infected–Removed if we allow for people to die from a disease and thus leave the population we are studying. Examples of diseases which fit the first category include chicken pox and influenza. Others that fit the second category where we may consider removals from a population would be HIV or the Bubonic Plague where many or most individuals die from contracting the disease. In order to keep things simple I concentrate on the first version of the model so that I may keep the population constant across time. This decision is entirely to keep things simple. At the end of this chapter I extend the model to one of a fluctuating population (with births and deaths) without much difficulty.

3.2 The SIR Model

In the introduction I mentioned that we are interested in the spread of an infectious disease where individuals may be susceptible to the disease, may be currently infected with the disease, or may be recovered and immune from the disease. I have three groups or states in which we can place individuals. In addition, the time dynamics will be of central importance in this section. So, again I want to consider the number of individuals in each category at each point in time. Let us begin with some notation.

$S_t =$ the number of susceptible individuals in the population at time t.
$I_t =$ the number of infected individuals in the population at time t.

R_t = the number of recovered individuals in the population at time t.
N = the population size.

Correspondingly define the three groups as fractions of the total population N in lower case.

$s_t = S_t/N$ (the susceptible fraction of the population at time t.)
$i_t = I_t/N$ (the infected fraction of the population at time t.)
$r_t = R_t/N$ (the recovered fraction of the population at time t.)

I use both of these sets of notation in the modeling process. Note that each individual in the population is in one of the three groups. Thus $S_t + I_t + R_t = N$ and $s_t + i_t + r_t = 1$.

3.2.1 Dynamics

If I think about the process of a disease that fits the SIR framework I have a flow of individuals from the susceptible group, to the infected group, and then, finally, to the recovered or removed group.

Susceptible → Infected → Recovered

An individual potentially moves from the susceptible to the infected group when she comes in contact with an infected person. What qualifies as a contact depends on the disease. For HIV a contact may be sexual contact or a blood transfusion. For influenza it may be walking within a few feet of an infected person that has recently coughed. Suppose that each infected person contacts γ individuals in each period of time on average. Every contact may not result in transmission of the disease. Perhaps only α percent of the contacts result in transmission. Thus the potential number of transmissions per period on average would be $\alpha\gamma$. Again, let us define this value as $\beta = \alpha\gamma$. β is the average number of transmissions possible from a given infected person in each period.

Now, remember that there are three groups in the population. Assume that individuals are mixed randomly. Contacts from an infective individual to a susceptible individual may result in a new infection. Or a contact may occur between an infective individual and another infective individual which results in nothing happening since the infective person is already infected. Finally, the contact may occur between an infective person and a recovered or immune person. In this case again nothing changes. Since only s_t percent of the population is susceptible each infective person generates only βs_t new infections each period. Each infective person recovers (or is removed/ dies) at some rate. Let the fraction of the infective group that recovers be κ.

We are now ready to describe the SIR process. Given the current state of the population in period t described by S_t, I_t and R_t I can write a series of difference equations that describe the motion of the system. First I describe the susceptible population. Begin period t with S_t individuals in the susceptible population. From

3.2 The SIR Model

this population we lose on average $\beta s_t I_t$ from the population through new infections. Thus in period $t+1$ we have:

$$S_{t+1} = S_t - \beta s_t I_t \tag{3.1}$$

The equation for the recovered population is similarly simple. Here a fraction κ of the infective population recovers and enters state R:

$$R_{t+1} = R_t + \kappa I_t \tag{3.2}$$

Finally, the change in the infective population is simply the increase in I from the flows out of state S and the flows out of state I and into state R described above to yield:

$$I_{t+1} = I_t + \beta s_t I_t - \kappa I_t = I_t(1 + \beta s_t - \kappa) \tag{3.3}$$

Similarly write each of these equations in terms of the population fractions:

$$s_{t+1} = s_t - \beta s_t i_t \tag{3.4}$$

Through similar reasoning:

$$r_{t+1} = r_t + \kappa i_t \tag{3.5}$$

and

$$i_{t+1} = i_t(1 + \beta s_t - \kappa) \tag{3.6}$$

Adding up these equations yields: $s_{t+1} + i_{t+1} + r_{t+1} = s_t + i_t + r_t = 1$.

3.3 Epidemic Threshold and Steady States

Note that we are above the epidemic threshold whenever $i_{t+1} > i_t$. This is equivalent to $s_t \beta > \kappa$. Whenever, this inequality holds we will be above the epidemic threshold and the number of infective individuals in the population will increase. This is the same as we found in the SIS model that we studied in the last chapter.

However, unlike the SIS model, there do not exist positive steady state levels of infected individuals in the SIR model if there is a constant population. To see why, first suppose that i_t is equal to 0. Then, from Eq. 3.6 you can see that $I_{t+1} = 0$. Thus if we start with no infective individuals in the population we stay there. This was true in the SIS model too. There has to be an initial positive number of infective individuals in the population in order for there to be more infective individuals. But in the SIS model there were other steady states as well. To see why those do not exist here, suppose that $i_t > 0$. I ask: will I_{t+1} be greater than, less than, or equal to I_t? The answer is either greater than or less than but never equal to (except in a special knife edge case that I will mention in a moment).

So, in most cases i_t will either be increasing or decreasing. How do we know which? We see from Eq. 3.6 that $i_{t+1} = i_t(1 + \beta s_t - \kappa)$. Let $\rho_t = 1 + \beta s_t - \kappa$. This is the epidemic threshold for the SIR model with a constant population. If ρ_t is greater than 1 then we are multiplying i_t by a number greater than 1 so $i_{t+1} > i_t$. The number of infected individuals is increasing; we are above the epidemic threshold. But if ρ_t is less than 1 we are multiplying i_t by a number less than 1 so $i_{t+1} < i_t$. The number of infected individuals is decreasing; we are below the epidemic threshold. Clearly any time $\rho_t > 1$ or $\rho_t < 1$ we are not at a steady state.

Now let us consider the possibility of $\rho_t = 1$ and show why, if we are at this point, it cannot persist. If $\rho_t = 1$ then either $i_t = 0$ or $\rho_{t+1} < \rho_t$. The first case is not interesting. This condition just means that there are no infective individuals so there is no possibility of anyone else being infected. The second case is more tricky. Let us again look at the definition of ρ_t, $\rho_t = 1 + \beta s_t - \kappa$ We see that there are three constants in the equation: 1, β and κ as well as one state variable s_t. Let us take another look at the equation for s_t given by Eq. 3.4. This equation is decreasing whenever $i_t > 0$. Thus if $i_t > 0$ ρ_t is decreasing for any $\beta > 0$. Thus there can never be a steady state where $\rho_t = 1$ and $i_t > 0$. Further if i_t is increasing it is doing so at a decreasing rate. And if i_t is decreasing it is doing so at an increasing rate. Combining these results indicates that the infected population will always disappear in the long run *if we have a constant population.*[1]

Now let us take a brief look at s_t and r_t. First let us look at s_t. We know that s_t is decreasing for $i_t > 0$. And we also know that i_t equals 0 in steady state. So, from this we can deduce that s_t will also reach a steady state value since it is constant if i_t is equal to 0 (see Eq. 3.4 to convince yourself.) Now, r_t is increasing for $i_t > 0$ and at steady state when $i_t = 0$. Like s_t, r_t will also reach a steady state value. What remains is to calculate what those steady state values are and the dynamic path to steady state given a set of initial conditions.

We could calculate this using analytical methods but we can most likely proceed quicker and with more understanding if we use computational techniques. This also will allow us to further expand our toolbox for understanding the rise and fall of epidemics.

3.4 Computational Analysis

To get a better feel for how the model behaves I now present a series of examples that were created using a simple spreadsheet. More sophisticated analysis can be done by creating these models in more sophisticated programming languages but much of the intuition for an SIR model can be realized with a very simple implementation. We begin by viewing the dynamic path of the epidemic. Suppose

---

[1] We discuss a model with a non-constant population at the end of the chapter.

3.4 Computational Analysis

that we have the following parameters that are known, $\kappa = 0.3333$, $\beta = 0.65$. We will simulate a population of 7,900,000 individuals (about the size of New York City when the Hong Kong Flu outbreak occurred in 1968.) We begin with one infected individual in the population and all other individuals in the susceptible category (no one is immune or vaccinated against the disease). Note that s_0 is very close to 1. Thus, for these parameter values $s_0\beta > \kappa$, we are above the epidemic threshold, and expect to see an outbreak of the infectious disease. The specific time dynamics are show in Fig. 3.1.

As you will note in the figure, it takes a fairly large number of periods for the outbreak to emerge in a noticeable fraction of the population. It isn't until about period 40 that we see a fraction of individuals infected approaching 1 % of the population. The epidemic then grows rapidly reaching a maximum fraction of infective individuals around period 55 when about 15 % of the population is infective. Also note that around these time periods the fraction of susceptible individuals is decreasing rapidly. Eventually the level of s_t drops to a level where $s_t < \kappa\beta$. At this point, we are below the epidemic threshold and the number of infective individuals begins to decrease. The epidemic then disappears fairly quickly. By period 75 the fraction of infected individuals is again less than 1 %. This is the general shape that you see in a traditional SIR epidemic such as influenza.

Note again, that the epidemic reaches a peak with 15 % of the population infected. However, this fact alone somewhat understates the size of the epidemic in the model. For a better understanding note the number of recovered individuals in the population. When the epidemic ends, about 80 % of the population is in the recovered group. This indicates that 80 % of the population has been infected during some period of the epidemic. Of course, this is a huge level. In a typical year around 20 % of the US population is infected with influenza. It would be rare for a typical seasonal disease to reach 80 % of the population. But, for the purposes of exposition I have chosen parameters to create a large epidemic so as to better display the shape of the time dynamics of an SIR epidemic.

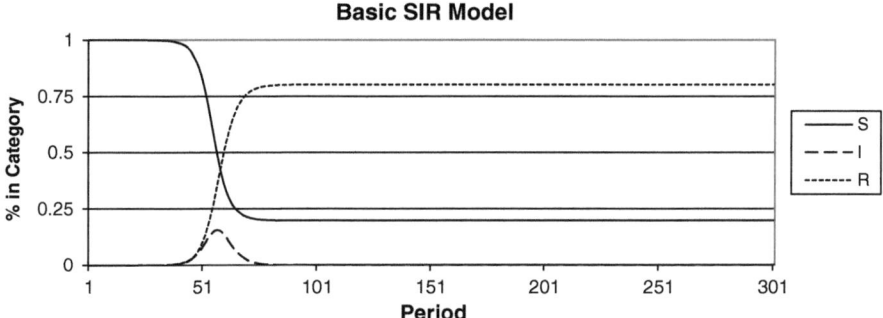

Fig. 3.1 Simple SIR model with $\beta = 0.65$ and $\kappa = 0.33$

If I begin changing parameters in the model one would see that an increase in β would increase the height of the spike in infections at the epidemic peak and a larger percentage of the population becomes infected over the entirety of the epidemic. Alternatively, if κ were to increase, so that individuals recover more quickly, the peak level of infections deceases and the number of total infections also decreases. In addition, as one can see in Fig. 3.2, where $\kappa = 0.45$, the peak of the epidemic occurs at a later time period. A quicker recovery rate, creates a smaller epidemic that takes a longer time to occur. It takes more time for the epidemic to build to noticeable levels because fewer individuals are infected early in the epidemic.

Finally, recall that there are two ways that people leave the infected pool. One is that the individual recovers. The other interpretation of the model is that people move to the R category because they are removed, or in other words, they die. One interpretation of our results above then is that epidemics that slowly kill people can be far more dangerous to the population as a whole than epidemics that kill people quickly. Thus if we compare some of the more sinister diseases of the past, epidemics such as the black plague (which usually resulted in death within one week of being infected) are potentially far less dangerous than something like HIV/ AIDS which can take years. Of course this is tempered by our current medical knowledge, treatment procedures, and understanding of the transmission of diseases. Yet, this is a result that many find surprising. If a disease removes its carriers quickly the disease is not likely to have a long life itself. Thus it sometimes occurs that diseases evolve to have weaker effects so that the virus or bacteria causing the disease can live longer and reproduce in larger numbers because of the smaller effects on the host. This may occur in multiple forms, it may simply allow the infected individual to live longer; or it may have smaller effects on the host allowing the host to remain more mobile and thus more able to infect other individuals.

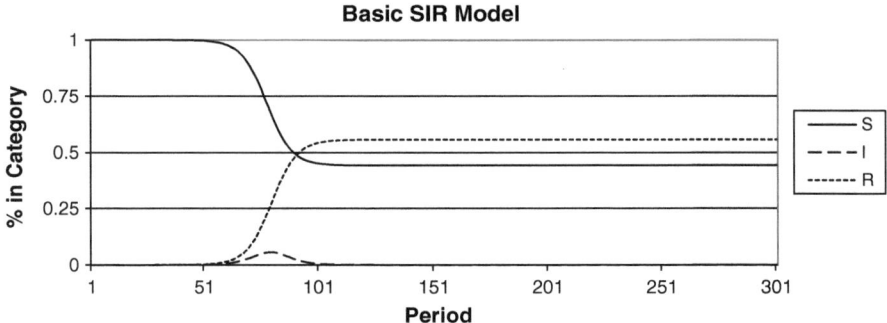

Fig. 3.2 Simple SIS model with higher κ, $\beta = 0.65$ and $\kappa = 0.45$

3.5 Herd Immunity

In the last section we saw one surprising fact, if people are going to die from an infectious disease it is better that they die fast *for the purpose of ending the epidemic*.[2] In this section we will see another potentially surprising fact: You do not need to immunize everyone in the population in order to prevent an epidemic.

To see this first recall that i_t is decreasing in the amount of susceptible individuals in the population. More exactly we saw above that if $1 + \beta s_t - \kappa$ is less than 1 the number of infected individuals will decrease. The social contact structure and the rate of removal, β and κ, are parameters of the social structure of the population and the disease of interest. As a social scientist there is nothing that I can do about κ since it is a function of biology and physiology which is under the purview of medical doctors and researchers. But as a social scientist or a public health official we do have some control over β since it is a function of the behavior of the population. We can make recommendations that sick children and workers stay home and not go to work or shopping when they are ill so that they do not infect others in the population. You may recall celebrating a day off from school as a young child because too many students were sick (assuming you were not one of the infected, of course!). We also can quarantine people for certain diseases. This would probably happen if a small pox outbreak occurred. In a later section of the book we will spend many words discussing specifically the contact structure of social populations and the potential effects of public policies designed to deal with epidemics.

But for now we will do something more simple. Let us assume that the medical researchers of the world have found a vaccine for our disease of interest. Further assume that if we immunize a person they are forever immune from catching the disease and thus from passing it on to someone else. Now, from a modeling perspective this essentially means that when a person is immunized they shift directly from the susceptible pool to the recovered pool without going through the infected phase. Instead of the following flows of people:

Susceptible $\rightarrow$ Infected $\rightarrow$ Recovered

we have:

Susceptible $\rightarrow$ Recovered

for those that are immunized.

Immunizing people from a disease is costly. There are the direct costs of producing and administering the dosage as well as indirect costs of providing information to the public. Thus we would like to be able to provide safety from disease at the lowest possible cost. What we will see in a moment is that we only have to immunize a fraction (many times a fraction much smaller than the total population) of the population in order to succeed in our task. Specifically we need

---

[2] Of course, sinister interpretations of this comment can be made which are not my intent.

to move enough people from the susceptible pool to the recovered (or in this case immune) pool such that the disease disappears of its own accord. In terms of our model we need to move enough people such that: $1 + \beta s_0 - \kappa < 1$. In other words we need to lower the reproduction number below one. Or to write it more directly the fraction of people that needs to be immunized is such that $s_0 < \kappa/\beta$. Thus you need to immunize $1 - \kappa/\beta$ percent of the susceptible pool. We should see that this makes intuitive sense. If κ is small that means that it takes longer to recover from infection and an infective person has more time to infect people. Thus as κ decreases $1 - \kappa/\beta$ increases; you need to inoculate a larger fraction of the population. As β increases, each infected person contacts more people in a given period, $1 - \kappa/\beta$ increases. Thus again you need to inoculate a larger fraction of the population.

Let's return to an example with parameters of $\beta = 6/10$ and $\kappa = 1/3$. We start the model with $I_0 = 1$; there is one infected individual. With these parameters we end up with about 75 % of the population becoming infected. We calculated that the number of people that you need to inoculate in order to stop an epidemic is $1 - \kappa/\beta$. In our example this is $1 - \frac{1/3}{6/10}$ or 4/9 of the population. In our example with 7,900,000 people this would be about 3.5 million vaccinations. So, in this exercise we have seen how one can use both analytical techniques and computational techniques to help gain a better understanding of a problem. The analytical techniques do a nice job of helping us to find the herd immunity threshold but do a poorer job of intuitively describing the dynamic story. The computational model does a great job of helping us easily see the dynamic story underlying the development and eventual demise of an SIR epidemic.

3.6 Non-Constant Populations

Before I close this chapter I should briefly consider the assumption of a constant population. Typically individuals enter and leave a population through a number of means, perhaps through immigration or even more simply by birth and death. I have not included any of these ideas in the model so far for the sake of simplicity. However, these can easily be incorporated into the equations above.

Suppose that each period n individuals (stated as a fraction of the total population) are born into the population and that m individuals (again stated as a fraction of the total population) die each period of random causes. Further let us assume that all newly born individuals are born into the susceptible population and that individuals are equally likely to die in any of the population groups. Again let us make a simplifying assumption. For simplicity, assume that $n = m$ so that the population size is constant.

The difference equations for s_t, i_t, and r_t with the birth and death rates included are:

3.6 Non-Constant Populations

$$s_{t+1} = s_t - \beta s_t i_t + n - m s_t \tag{3.7}$$

$$i_{t+1} = i_t + \beta s_t i_t - \kappa i_t - m i_t = (1 + \beta s_t - \kappa - m) i_t \tag{3.8}$$

$$r_{t+1} = r_t + \kappa i_t - m r_t \tag{3.9}$$

Note that these equations are identical to those without birth and death except for the last term in each case.

What you should be able to see with a little work is that if there are enough births and deaths in the population there can be steady state levels of the infected population greater than 0.

With a little algebra, and the assumption that $n = m$ one can find that the steady state levels of s^*, i^*, and r^* are:

$$s^* = \frac{\kappa + m}{\beta} \tag{3.10}$$

$$i^* = \frac{(\beta - \kappa - m)m}{\beta(\kappa + m)} \tag{3.11}$$

$$r^* = \frac{(\beta - \kappa - m)\kappa}{\beta(\kappa + m)} \tag{3.12}$$

One can see from the i^* equation that you need $m > 0$ and $\beta - \kappa - m > 0$ in order for there to be a positive steady state. This implies that any sufficiently small level of m greater than zero implies that there is a positive fraction of the population infective in steady state. Also note that the equation for i^* is quadratic in m. As m increases from 0 the steady state level of infective individuals will increase. But, once m gets too large, the resulting epidemic is smaller; And, for $m > \beta - \kappa$ we again return to the case of $i^* = 0$ in the long run. This occurs because the turnover in the population is so quick as to not allow the infective population to last long enough so that we are above the epidemic threshold. Each infective person is removed prior to infecting one or more persons on average. In Figs. 3.3 and 3.4 you can see two examples for different levels of β. For high β, Fig. 3.3, the product of the transmission rate and contact rate is high enough that a non-zero steady state level of infective individuals can be sustained even with very high turnover in the population. However, note that the steady state level is decreasing past a turnover rate of about 4 million people per period. For a lower level of β the size of the steady state epidemic is much lower, as one would expect, and the level of turnover where the $i^* = 0$ steady state becomes the unique steady state occurs with a much lower turnover in the population. The practical relevance of having turnover rates in the population high enough that an epidemic is stopped may be slight. But, one should be aware that increasing turnover can both lead to more infections in steady state or less depending on other parameters of an infectious disease of interest.

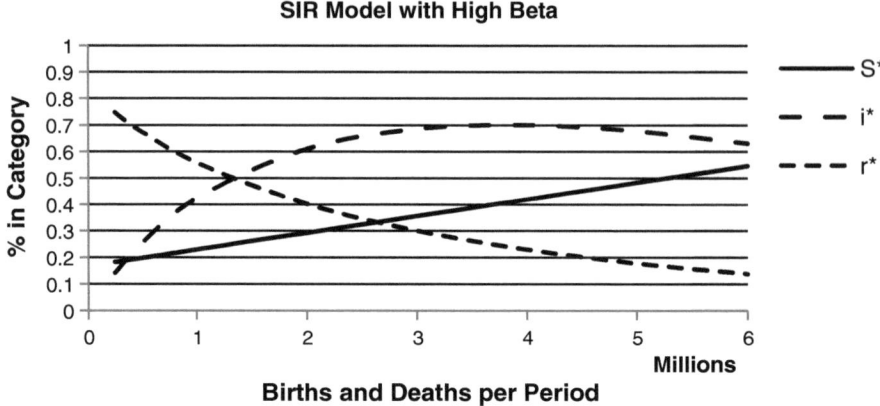

Fig. 3.3 Steady state levels of an SIR model with population turnover and $\beta = 2.0$

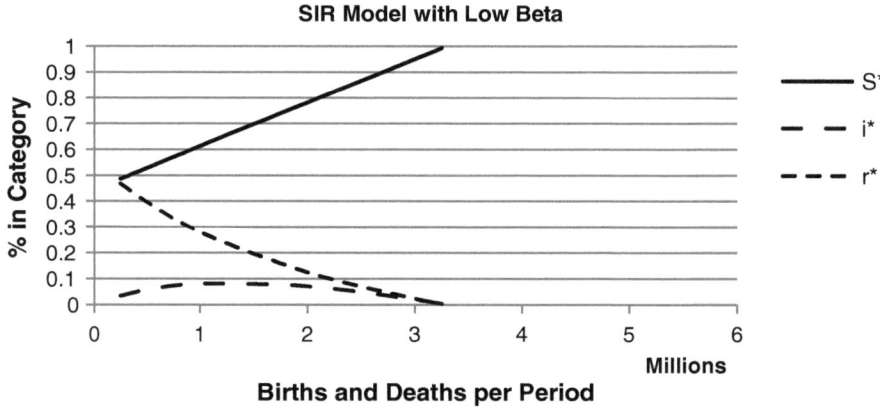

Fig. 3.4 Steady state levels of an SIR model with population turnover and $\beta = 0.75$

As a final note in this chapter, note Fig. 3.5, in particular the levels of r and i once the steady state is reached. Although i is relatively low, about 3 % of the population, r is large, about 80 % of the population. This result harkens back to our earlier discussion of the relationship between the peak in infections and the total number of people infected in the base SIR epidemic. Here, even though the steady state level of infections is low, most of the population is eventually infected and subsequently recovers. Because of this most of the new infections will come from individuals recently introduced into the population (fairly new births). This should remind you of childhood disease such as chicken pox. Prior to the chicken pox vaccine being developed, many if not most children in the U.S. were infected at some point in their young lives and recovered to be immune (in most cases) to future infections. This is the product of the general dynamic trajectory of an SIR

3.6 Non-Constant Populations

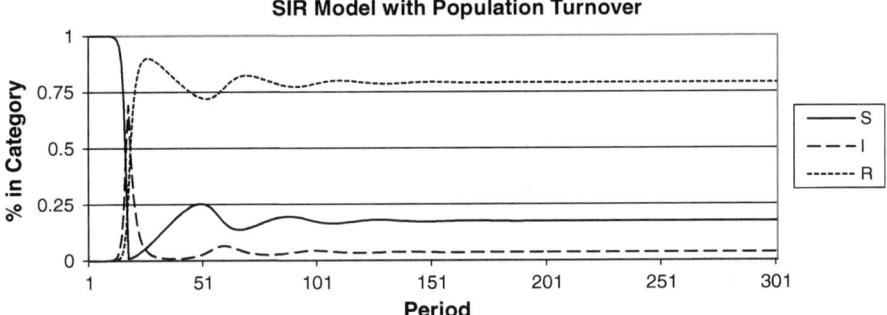

Fig. 3.5 SIR model with population turnover

model in steady state. With the basics of some simple epidemiological models covered we are now ready to introduce some economic methodology in the next section of the book.

Part II
Merging Economics and Epidemiology

Chapter 4
Economic Modeling and Epidemiology

Having provided an introduction to some basic epidemiological modeling, I next present some basic economic principles that result from these models. Namely, I want to discuss how the economic concepts of positive and negative externalities as well as marginal changes can be used to better understand public health policy. I begin by introducing the economic concept of utility that the reader may have seen in an introductory economics course and the concept of a value function which calculates the utility of an individual being in a particular category or state of interest. I then show how this formulation can be used to state externalities and inform decision making at both an individual and public level.

4.1 Economic Utility

Economists use the concept of utility as a measure of the overall well-being of an individual or of an action taken by an individual. Essentially, the more "happiness" an individual derives from some action or decision, the more utility the individual has received. Note that the utility of an individual may encompass more than just her own intrinsic happiness or well-being. An individual may be better off if a friend or spouse is happier too. Thus someone may increase her utility by doing a favor for a friend even though it incurs a cost on the individual. Thus utility can accommodate preferences for others. Economists also discuss two distinct and important measures of utility. One is termed *Total Utility* and represents the total amount of well-being an individual has from a series of actions or decisions. For instance, I can discuss my total utility from consuming 4 slices of pizza, 2 veggie burgers, and a salad over my seven lunches this week. However much well-being I have derived from these meals is my total utility from lunch this week. Economists also discuss the concept of marginal utility. Marginal utility is measured as the change in total utility from consuming one more unit of a good, service, or abstractly "thing." For instance suppose that I am currently at 60 units of utility after my lunches from Sunday until Friday and I eat a salad on Saturday which brings my total utility to 65. My total utility has increased by five units of utility by eating the salad. Thus I would say that the marginal utility of my salad is five.

Note that so far I have not stated the units of measure for utility. Because utility is an abstract concept I am free to define utility in any units I like. For instance I could measure utility in terms of some internal measure of "happiness" and claim that my lunch today gave me eight units of happiness. Of course this would not be a very useful way of stating things because another person cannot directly relate to what eight units of happiness really means. Is eight large or small? We cannot tell from the outside. I could also measure utility in something more concrete. For instance I could say that my lunch today of a slice of pizza gave me four oranges of utility. And, what I would mean by this is that I would be indifferent between having eaten my pizza slice or four oranges. Note that this gives you something more concrete to judge (you know how much well being you would gain from eating four oranges) but you still would not be able to fully understand exactly what amount of well-being I gained from my lunch because you do not know what well-being I would gain from four oranges, other than it is equivalent to a slice of pizza for lunch today. What you would know though, is that if you have five oranges tomorrow, and would prefer a slice of pizza to your five oranges that you could trade me five oranges for a slice of pizza which I view as equivalent to four oranges. (Of course, this assumes that I like five oranges better than four, which should not be unreasonable even to non-economists!) Similarly, if I told you that a slice of pizza is worth $3 to me, you could offer me $4 and I would take it. Similarly, if the pizza was worth $5 to you, you would be happy to pay me $4. We would both be better off if you gave me $4 for my slice of pizza. Thus, we could measure utility in terms of dollars, oranges, or anything else for that matter. However, since the costs of things are usually measured in terms of money, it is common for economists to measure utility in terms of money too. If the price of something is $x and I get more marginal utility from it than $x, then I should buy it. Now, the danger here, is that if we think of utility as well-being or happiness, and we measure utility in money, one can erroneously think that economists think of happiness and money as the same thing. But, note this is not the case. Money is simply an easy to use abstract unit. Economists could just as easily think of utility as measured in oranges or slices of pizza as money.

4.2 Utility and Epidemic Modeling

In the context of this book we are interested in using the concept of utility to discuss the economics of infectious disease. Specifically I first discuss the utility of being in various states related to the infectious disease. Let U_j be the utility of being in state j at some period of time, where j indicates one of the previously discussed states such as susceptible, infected, or recovered. I make the general assumption that the utility of being infected is smaller than the utility of being

4.2 Utility and Epidemic Modeling

susceptible or recovered. Further, I assume that the utility of being susceptible is the same as that of being recovered; essentially I assume that if you are feeling well, then you derive the same level of utility whether recovered or susceptible. Of course, there may be exceptions to this statement in practice. Perhaps after recovering there are continuing symptoms or health problems that persist after recovery. Or, it may be that one has more peace of mind having acquired some virus, surviving it, and knowing that you cannot be infected again. In this book I will ignore these potential subtleties and generally assume that $U_s = U_r > U_i$.

I can consider two types of models as we did previously. In an SIS model, where a recovered individual becomes susceptible, the susceptible and recovered states are identical. In the SIR model, the only difference between being recovered and susceptible is that a recovered individual cannot be infected again. In this chapter we will concentrate on the intuition for an SIR model and one can easily extend this intuition and modeling practice to an SIS model if you choose.

The next tool we need is something economists call a value function. A value function incorporates the various costs and benefits of an individual being in a specified state. So, for instance if one is susceptible to a disease the benefits to an individual are the utility that she currently has, and the costs are the possibility of becoming infected (weighted by the probability of being infected). So, one could write the value of being in state S as:

$$V_s = U_s - \pi C_i \tag{4.1}$$

where, U_s is defined above, π is the probability of being infected and C_i is the cost of the infection. We will define C_i as the difference in utility between feeling well in state S (or state R) and receiving the lower utility in state I over the period of the infection. (There may also be some monetary cost of being in state I for treatment or missed time from work, but we will assume that these values are already netted out in terms of the difference in utility in order to simplify notation.) Thus we can write $C_i = U_s - U_i$.

Following, we can write the value of being in state I as $V_i = U_i$ and $V_r = U_r = U_s$. In both of these cases in an SIR model, once infected or recovered there is no chance of returning to the infected state.

4.3 The Economics of Prevention

With a basic set-up in place I can begin discussing the economics of prevention. As an example there may be a vaccine available that moves one from the susceptible state to the recovered state (assuming the vaccine is effective.) Or, one could similarly discuss other prevention measures such as quarantines that limit the number of interactions an individual has. As another example, one could choose to abstain from some behaviors that put you at risk for infection. The cost of this behavior would be the lost opportunity of utility from the activity from which you abstain. There are numerous other examples that one can think of but, for the most part, as an introduction, we will work with the idea of a vaccine as our primary example.

Suppose a fully effective vaccine is available for a disease of interest. (If the vaccine is not fully effective one could simply insert a probability weighting to the equations below and carry out the analysis without any additional differences.) Further suppose that the cost of the vaccine is stated as c_v. This cost of the vaccine will include any monetary cost directly associated with the vaccine (any direct payment or insurance co-pay etc) as well as any utility based cost (cost of lost time to go to the doctor, inconvenience, or even overcoming a fear of needles!) We can use this set-up to consider two items of interest: First, under what circumstances will an individual choose to be vaccinated? Second, if we as a society could make a decision for every individual, who (or how many) people would we choose to vaccinate? We begin with the first question.

4.3.1 Individual Prevention Decisions

If a vaccine is available, a susceptible individual faces the following decision: Do I choose to accept the vaccine and pay the cost of being vaccinated or do I forgo the vaccine and risk being infected. In making this decision one must compare the value functions associated with each decision. If one forgoes the vaccine he is simply in the susceptible state which has a value of $V_s = U_s - \pi C_i$. On the other hand if one chooses to be vaccinated he moves to the value of state R but also has to pay the cost of being vaccinated, c_v. Thus the vaccine choice has the following value: $V_r - c_v = U_s - c_v$. The individual then needs to make a comparison of those two values. If $U_s - c_v > U_s - \pi C_i$ the individual should choose to be vaccinated. This inequality will hold if $c_v < \pi C_i$. Simply put, the individual will choose to be vaccinated if the cost of the vaccine is less than the probability of being infected multiplied by the cost of infection.

4.3.2 Public Prevention Decisions

The individual prevention decision was straight-forward, simple, and intuitive. Thinking more broadly, as economists and public officials are well aware, individual decisions do not always coincide with the best interests of society. This occurs when individual decisions have effects on other members of society. Economists call these situations externalities. Sometimes externalities lead to better outcomes for society and sometimes to worse outcomes. As examples, smoking and pollution are often cited as examples of negative externalities. If someone chooses to smoke others may be forced to inhale the smoker's second hand smoke. Thus the choice to smoke forces others to incur costs that they did not

4.3 The Economics of Prevention

choose. On the other hand, sometimes the choices we make lead to benefits for others in society. For instance, maintaining your lawn and planting flowers in front of your house is an individual decision that you make. But, your neighbors are likely to enjoy seeing your well-manicured lawn and thus derive some benefit and utility from your decision to plant a beautiful flower bed. Two standard results in introductory economics state that, because individuals primarily consider only their own costs and benefits when making a decision and ignore the costs and benefits of others: first, decisions which lead to negative externalities occur too often (because the costs of society are not fully considered); second, decisions that lead to positive externalities occur to infrequently (because the benefits of society are not fully considered.)

Now, suppose that you could act as an overseer of all vaccine decisions in society with the goal of making the best decision for the entire population. Economists often call this the social planner's decision or the social planner's problem. The distinction between this decision and the individual level decision is that the social planner needs to consider the possibility that a non-vaccinated individual will infect others in the population who will then bear the cost of being infected. Thus infections create a negative externality in society. Specifically, if individual A becomes infected he will infect, on average, β individuals, where β is again the product of the transmission and contact rate, $\alpha\gamma$. (Note that I am neglecting the time subscript here for notational simplicity.) Thus, as a first approximation, one may think that the decision rule for a social planner is: $c_v < (1 + \beta s)\pi C_i$.

However, this solution has a few problems. First, as previously discussed, s will decrease as more vaccines occur and as more infections take place. As a matter of timing, the need to vaccinate individuals decreases as an epidemic spreads because there are fewer susceptible people to infect. The good news here is that, from a mathematical perspective, if it is not worthwhile to vaccinate an individual in the first period it will not be worthwhile to vaccinate them at a later time period. Second, the term βs overstates the number of infections that would be prevented if the individual were to be effectively vaccinated. The logic lies in the fact that individuals are connected to more than one person. If individual A receives her vaccine she cannot pass an infection to individual B. But, individual B could be infected by another contact, say, individual C. Vaccinating A guarantees that B will not be infected by A but not by someone else in the population. Thus the social planner needs to know the true number of infections that vaccinating an individual prevents in the population. Define this value as the *marginal infections*.

Definition 1 The marginal infections of individual j, denoted m_j, are the decrease in infections that would occur if individual j were to be removed from the population.

The marginal infections can be a complicated entity. For instance, m_j will depend on the size of the epidemic, the number of vaccinations performed in the population, the overall structure of contacts in the population (including the contacts of j, the contacts of j's contacts, and so on...). Obviously, this value would require a complicated calculation. If one has knowledge of the structure of contacts in a population or if one is willing to make simplifying assumptions about that contact structure it can be calculated using simple computer simulations. As an example, in the spreadsheet examples above, one could simply remove one individual from the susceptible category and view how the number in infected individuals changes. For now, we will assume that m_j can be calculated and proceed with the economic analysis.

With the term marginal infections defined, we can now write the social planner's problem as: vaccinate individual j if $c_v < (1+m_j)\pi C_i$.

If we compare this decision to the individual decision problem you will note that they are the same except for a term, $m_j \pi C_i$ on the right hand side. This is the externality that an individual creates if she chooses not to be vaccinated. As we can see from the problem, a social planner will choose to vaccinate more individuals than will choose to be vaccinated on their own as long as m_j is greater than 0. Vaccinating individuals creates a positive externality in society as more people are protected from being infected than just the individual vaccinated.

The most common way to create efficiency with a positive externality is to provide a subsidy. This subsidy could be in the form of providing the vaccine at a lower cost or it could be provided as a direct transfer to recipients. Suppose that an agency pays a vaccine recipient a monetary amount of T when receiving the vaccine. The recipient then adds this amount to the right hand side of his decision rule to get: $c_v < \pi C_i + T$. If T is set equal to the amount of the externality, namely $T = m_j \pi C_i$ then the individual decision problem and the social planner's decision problem yield the same level of vaccinations.

There are, however, a few difficulties in calculating this subsidy. So far we have not discussed any kind of heterogeneity in the population. Most notably, we have assumed the number of contacts and the probability of being infected are the same for everyone. Nor have we discussed the costs of infection and vaccination, C_i and c_v which could also vary across individuals. To be more specific, suppose that we set T as a uniform subsidy payment available to everyone. If there is heterogeneity in individuals, we will still mis-allocate the vaccine. To see this we define two concepts. First,

Definition 2 A vaccine subsidy is said to be *incentive compatible* for individual j if $c_{v,j} < \pi_j C_{i,j} + T$.

This condition simply means that individual j will accept the subsidy and vaccine for the various parameters associated with their decision. Second,

Definition 3 A vaccine subsidy is said to be *cost effective* for the social planner if $T < m_j \pi_j C_{i,j}$.

This condition means that the amount of the subsidy should be less than the externality.

4.3 The Economics of Prevention

Ideally a social planner would like all cost effective subsidies to also be incentive compatible. If this was the case, each individual that the social planner would like to be vaccinated, will also accept the subsidy and be vaccinated. For this to be true the probability of infection must be sufficiently large for an individual to accept the subsidy and the marginal infections created must be sufficiently large for the subsidy to be cost effect. Specifically,

$$\pi_j > \frac{c_{v_*} - T}{C_{i,j}} \quad (4.2)$$

and,

$$m_j > \frac{T}{\pi_j C_{i,j}} \quad (4.3)$$

Of course, with a uniform subsidy T this will not always be the case. Thus it may be necessary to target the size of the subsidy depending on specific levels of probability of infection and the level of marginal infections and tailor the subsidy to the specific level of marginal infections, and costs of infection and vaccine appropriate for individual j.

Finally, note, as mentioned earlier, that the externality and the level of marginal infections will decrease as more individuals are vaccinated. Specifically, as the number of vaccinations approaches the level where herd immunity is reached, the marginal infections of all individuals approach 0. At this point, the individual decision problem and the social planner's decision problem converge. However, note that, when this level of vaccinations is reached, the infectious disease is eliminated. Recall that we would not want to vaccinate individual j unless $c_v < (1 + m_j)\pi C_i$. Similarly in the individual decision problem, individual j will only choose to be vaccinated if $c_v < \pi C_i$. Because m_j and π approach 0, in both decision problems there is some level of vaccinations where we will stop vaccinating individuals as long as there is a positive cost of vaccination, c_v. This leads one to believe that complete disease eradication will not come about from individual decisions and will not come about from short-sighted public health subsidies. If a more expansive model is created where the government agency is providing the subsidy, it may be worth-while to spend more now to eradicate the disease in order to spend less in the future in order to again reach herd immunity.[1]

4.3.3 Costs and Benefits of Public Health Decisions

One of the standard hallmarks of economics is comparison of costs and benefits. Epidemiology gives another example of this procedure. For instance in the

---

[1] The point that disease eradication is unlikely to come about without policy intervention was fist made in Geoffard and Philipson 1997.

analysis of the opening chapters we discussed how the product of the transmission rate and the contact rate, $\alpha\gamma$, (along with the recovery rate, κ) play a primary role in the spread of an infectious disease. We also combined this product with the idea of reproduction number and discussed how, lowering the reproduction number below 1 would result in the end of an epidemic. Or, conversely, how using vaccinations or other publicly available strategies to keep $R_0 < 1$ would prevent an epidemic from starting (ie, leaving us below the epidemic threshold with herd immunity). Of course, when this practice is costly we want to be able to use funds in an efficient manner. In economics we can characterize this problem in two different ways. In the first there is a fixed budget available for public health expenditures and we wish to use the budget in the most effective way possible. In the second, we have a specific goal in mind, such as placing a population below the epidemic threshold, and we want to do so by the least costly means possible.

In the following discussion I use the following general notation and assumptions. First I assume that there is a known transmission rate and a known interaction rate. Further both of these terms can be altered by the use of money to change behavior. For instance, it may be that actions can be taken to limit the interactions of individuals on public transit thereby lowering γ. Or, it may be possible to improve the nutritional content of food and thereby improve immune system strength and lower α. Similarly, a government may provide a subsidy for a partially effective vaccine again lowering the expected transmission rate. For our purposes let us suppose that we know the functional form for how money spent changes these parameters. Let them be $\alpha(x)$ and $\gamma(y)$ where x and y are the amounts spent on lowering the transmission and interaction rates. $\alpha(x)$ is decreasing in x and $\gamma(y)$ is decreasing in y: $\frac{d\alpha(x)}{dx} < 0$ and $\frac{d\gamma(y)}{dy} < 0$. Further suppose that there is a fixed budget B that can be spent on these two items. We can now specify the two specific economic problems at hand.

First, suppose that we intend to spend the entire budget, B. The question we want to ask is, how do we minimize the spread of this infectious disease? The answer to this question involves minimizing the product of the transmission and contact rates subject to the constraint that we do not spend more than B. Specifically:

$$Min_{x,y}\ \alpha(x)\gamma(y) \text{ subject to } x+y \leq B.$$

In the best case scenario, the minimization problem would leave us below the epidemic threshold and the infectious disease would disappear. But even if this is not the case, lowering some combination of the transmission and contact rate, even if we stay above the epidemic threshold, would lower the steady state level of infections in an SIS model or would lower the size of the outbreak in an SIR model. The economic question then becomes whether the benefits of this lower level of prevalence outweigh the costs of B.

Additionally, if the outbreak is a new virus and the minimization yields a level of R_0 less than 1, it may be optimal or efficient to not spend all of the budget B. In this case all we need to do is keep the product of the transmission rate and contact

4.3 The Economics of Prevention

rate below 1 and an epidemic never starts. These ideas yield our second characteristic problem which is to minimize the expenses subject to keeping the reproduction number below 1.

$$Min_{x,y}\, x+y \quad \text{subject to} \quad \alpha(x)\gamma(y) \leq 1 \quad \text{and} \quad x+y \leq B.$$

Note that this problem may not always have a valid solution. It may be that the only levels of x and y that yield $R_0 < 1$ are levels that yield $x+y > B$. In this case we simply return to the previously stated problem where you minimize R_0 subject to the budget constraint in order to lower but not eliminate the impact of the epidemic (because it is not possible without a larger budget).

Reference

Geoffard P-Y, Philipson T (1997) Disease eradication: public vs. private vaccination. Am Econ Rev 87(1):222–230

Chapter 5
Econometrics and Epidemiology

One goal of creating a model is to organize thoughts, ideas, or assumptions into a coherent form so as to draw out the logical implications of the basic premises of the model. A second reason to create a model is to empirically test a hypothesis or empirically measure the magnitude of some effect. The goal of this chapter is to demonstrate the usefulness of precise modeling for empirical estimation.

Some of the comparative statics results of the opening chapters may have come as little surprise. For instance, recall that the steady state level of susceptible individuals in the SIS model was $\bar{s} = \frac{\kappa}{\alpha\gamma}$ and the steady state level for infective individuals was $\bar{i} = 1 - \frac{\kappa}{\alpha\gamma}$. As the recovery rate increases the steady state level of susceptible individuals increases and the steady state level of infective individuals decreases. Or, as either transmission or contact rates increase, the steady state level of susceptible individuals decreases and the steady state level of infective individuals increases. This may have been what you would guess without the modeling exercise carried out in Chap. 2. Yet, as I show below, this precise modeling helps greatly in understanding the relationship among variables and in performing valid empirical estimation.

Suppose that you have a data set containing information on an infectious disease of interest and you know the disease fits the SIS framework. Specifically suppose that you have information on the fraction of individuals who are susceptible and infective as well as an estimate of the key parameters of the disease κ, α, and γ. These last three items are somewhat of a simplification. Take the contact rate, γ, for example. This contact rate may depend on demographic variables in the population, access to public transportation, population density, etc. And, you could use those directly or you could use them to estimate the contact rate γ. There would be similar underlying variables that would determine the transmission rate and the recovery rate. In this exercise I will keep things as simple as possible and suppose that we know (or have already estimated) these parameter values directly. So, we may have a data set that looks like Table 5.1.

In the data set, suppose that there are 10 regions (countries or geographic areas). The values for κ, α, and γ are known in each region and given in Table 5.1. Suppose that these three parameters determine the level of infective and

Table 5.1 An example SIS data set

Region	s	i	κ	α	γ	ε	Model = $\frac{\kappa}{\alpha\gamma}$
1	0.250	0.750	0.288	0.375	3.131	0.005	0.245
2	0.341	0.659	0.393	0.387	2.849	−0.016	0.357
3	0.428	0.572	0.360	0.297	2.841	0.002	0.426
4	0.541	0.459	0.389	0.232	3.131	0.007	0.534
5	0.195	0.805	0.181	0.311	3.153	0.010	0.185
6	0.225	0.775	0.212	0.289	3.324	0.004	0.220
7	0.397	0.603	0.298	0.253	3.092	0.016	0.381
8	0.219	0.781	0.184	0.295	2.769	−0.006	0.225
9	0.428	0.572	0.393	0.312	2.909	−0.005	0.433
10	0.365	0.635	0.382	0.378	2.859	0.011	0.354

susceptible individuals in the population according to the steady state equation $\bar{s} = \frac{\kappa}{\alpha\gamma}$ with some small amount of error. The error is given by ϵ in the table. Thus to get the observed level of susceptible individuals in region i one calculates $s_i = \frac{\kappa}{\alpha\gamma} + \epsilon_i$. In the table for region 1 this would be $s_1 = 0.245 + 0.005 = 0.250$. The idea is that there is either some small amount of measurement error in the parameter or category variables or there is some small amount of idiosyncratic features that slightly differentiate the 10 regions.

We will assume that a researcher or public health official takes the approach of knowing s, i, κ, α, and γ. Further the researcher expects that κ is positively related to s and α and γ are negatively related to s. The researcher's goal is to understand how the three parameters are related to the category variable s and more importantly how the magnitude of the three parameters change s. As an example, the researcher may have money that can be used in one of three ways (1) lower contact rates in the population, (2) distribute nutritional supplements (providing for faster recovery), or (3) distribute a means to lower transmission rates (perhaps soap for better hand hygiene.) The question that is then faced is which lever should be used to best increase the level of susceptible individuals (lower the level of infective individuals)?

To answer this question one needs to know how much a change in each of κ, α, and γ change the level of s (and thereby i). So, suppose that the researcher runs the following linear regression $s_i = \beta_0 + \beta_1\kappa + \beta_2\alpha + \beta_3\gamma$ using the data above. The results are shown in Table 5.2. The regression has an $R^2 = 0.988$. From looking at the results, one might expect that this is a reasonable description of the effects of the three parameters and further, expect that it would be acceptable to base policies on these results. First, the fit of the regression and the data is very high (as measured by R^2). Second, the coefficients on all of the independent variables have the expected sign indicating that an increase in κ will increase the fraction of susceptible individuals and lower the fraction of infective individuals, and that an increase in α or γ will lower the fraction of susceptible individuals and increase the fraction of infective individuals. If all you had was information on s, i, κ, α, and γ this seems like a reasonable set of results on which to base policy.

5 Econometrics and Epidemiology

Table 5.2 Simple OLS regression results—misspecified

Variable	Coefficient	Std. error	t-stat	p-value
intercept	0.439	0.116	3.775	0.009
κ	1.189	0.062	19.080	0.000
α	−1.209	0.104	−11.584	0.000
γ	−0.029	0.032	−0.925	0.390

Looking closer at the results and knowing how the underlying data was created begins to reveal some problems however. Note that the absolute value of the coefficient on κ and α is about the same; indicating that a change of the same magnitude in one of these underlying parameters will have the same effect on s (although in the opposite direction.) Also note by looking at the standard errors, t-stats, or p-values, that the coefficients on these two parameters are significantly different from 0. Now look at the coefficient on γ. As already mentioned, it is negative, which is expected. Also, note however that the coefficient on γ would be considered not significantly different from 0 at any typically accepted level of confidence. Essentially, this leads one to believe that γ does not have any effect on s or i. As we know, this is incorrect. The denominator of the equation used to create s contains the product $\alpha\gamma$. Thus, the effect of γ is equivalent to the effect of α. Yet our regression is telling us to ignore it. From a policy perspective, the regression would tell us to spend all of our resources on increasing the recovery rate or decreasing the transmission rate but to ignore the contacts in the population. Obviously, given that we created the data, we know this to be incorrect. In addition, this specification also yields a non-zero and statistically significant intercept term. Again, this is incorrect.

So, what went wrong? Directly, the model that produced the regression results is mis-specified. We did not use the correct underlying model when we ran our regressions. Yet, the regression we ran looks a lot like most of those that you see in academic papers, and policy estimations. It is common to line-up a linear set of independent variables on the right hand side of an OLS equation, run the regression and interpret the results much as we did with this example (good fit, expected signs, check statistical significance, and accept the results.) And, unless you know the true underlying relationships in the world you will not realize your mistake because everything looks fine and intuitive.

The problem does not go away if you begin adding other features to the regression model without being more precise with your modeling. For instance if you use the same data again and run a regression with an $\alpha * \gamma$ interaction term to the previous regression you will still get very misleading results as can be seen in Table 5.3. Again you would get a very good fit, but in this case only the coefficient on κ is significantly different from 0.

What is needed is better modeling of the process that you are trying to estimate. Specifically, you need to run the regression as $\beta_0 + \beta_1 \frac{\kappa}{\alpha\gamma}$. These results are shown in Table 5.4. If one does this, you get $\beta_0 = 0.004$ (combined with the standard errors reveals β_0 not significantly different from 0) and $\beta_1 = 0.997$ (statistically different from 0 for the resulting standard errors). This is the correct relationship.

Table 5.3 Simple OLS regression results—mis-specified model

Variable	Coefficient	Std. error	t-stat	p-value
intercept	0.985	0.849	1.160	0.298
κ	1.214	0.076	15.978	0.000
α	−3.038	2.819	−1.078	0.330
γ	−0.212	0.284	−0.748	0.488
$\alpha * \gamma$	0.607	0.935	0.649	0.545

Table 5.4 Simple OLS regression results—correct model

Variable	Coefficient	Std. error	t-stat	p-value
intercept	0.004	0.010	0.362	0.727
$\frac{\kappa}{\alpha\gamma}$	0.997	0.029	34.118	0.000

The point of this chapter is to emphasize that one needs to be very careful when basing policy prescriptions on simple linear regressions. Simply lining up a set of potential contributing independent variables in a regression is unlikely to lead to meaningful and accurate results even in a simple situation like the one presented in this example. Instead, one needs to first carefully model the phenomenon of interest in order to have a correctly specified estimation that will be meaningful and accurate for policy analysis.

Part III
An Introduction to Social Interactions

Chapter 6
Interaction Networks: An Introduction

In the proceeding chapters I have presented introductory models of infectious disease. So, far the important variables we have studied include the transmission rate, the recovery rate, and the per period number of contacts of individuals in the population. As a social scientist, there is little that I can say about the first of these two items. A transmission rate or a recovery rate are going to be influenced by the biological and medical advancements of society, not by the workings of an economist! The third item however, falls directly into the realm of social science—individual contacts. In the social sciences there have been great advancements in our understanding of social networks over the past two decades. We better understand how people interact and how various social network structures impact everything from the diffusion of new products to rates of learning, to the propagation of a financial crises, and of course, to our topic of interest, the spread of infectious disease.

So far the epidemic models I have presented have been very simple; I have assumed that people interact randomly in a population so that each person is equally likely to interact with any other person. Of course, this assumption is not an accurate portrayal of the world in which we live. The people we come in contact with are determined by many things: Some are immutable characteristics like age, gender, race, and ethnicity. Others are characteristics that individuals choose (at least in part) such as where one lives or favorite recreational pastimes. Then there are other elements that fall somewhere in between like socio-economic status which is partly determined by choice and partly determined by the various opportunities that are presented to us throughout our lives. What social scientists have found over the past few years though is that there are many properties of social interactions that transcend these various dimensions. There are properties of social networks that tend to be true regardless of where one falls in the list of individual characteristics above. In this section of the book, I provide a description of these general network characteristics and discuss the implications for the spread of infectious disease. I begin by answering the question, what is a Network?

Mathematically a network is a collection of "nodes" that are connected by edges (sometimes referred to as links or connections). In Fig. 6.1 there are five nodes labeled A, B, C, D, and E. Nodes are connected together by edges. There are six edges in the figure: There are edges from A to B, B to C, C to D, C to E, D to E and E to A. An arrow on the end of an edge indicates direction. Edges with a direction are termed "directed edges."

Edges may also be undirected as in Fig. 6.2. Here, there are again five nodes but there are only four edges which connect A to C, B to E, D to E and E to A. And because the edges are not directed they also indicate that the edges connect C to A, E to B, E to D and A to E. As an example, think of a one-way street as a directed edge and a two-way street as an undirected edge.

Each individual node in a network also has some characteristics related to the network. For instance the *degree* of a node is defined as the number of edges connected to it. In Fig. 6.2 the degree of node A is two, the degree of node B is one, the degree of node C is one, the degree of node D is one and the degree of node E is three. If the network is directed, as in Fig. 6.1, the node has both an in-degree (the number of edges pointing to it,) and an out-degree (the number of edges emanating from it.) In Fig. 6.1 nodes A, B and D all have in-degree of one and out-degree of one. Node C has in-degree of one and out-degree of two. Node E has in-degree of two and out-degree of one.

We can think of almost any real-world set of connections as a network. For instance you may quickly think of networks of computers in your office or school. Each computer or terminal is a node on a network and each connection between terminals is an edge. Similarly you can also think of the world wide web as a network. Each individual web page is a node and each link between pages is an edge. Networks also exist in biology and the environment. We could think of the

Fig. 6.1 A simple directed network

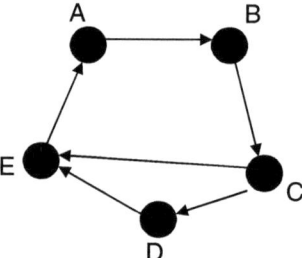

Fig. 6.2 A simple undirected network

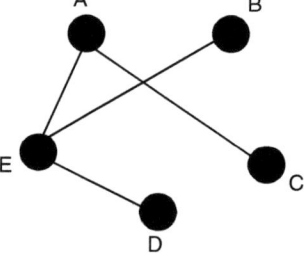

structure of which animals eat which other animals as a network. For instance humans eat fish, cows, chickens, etc. Thus we could connect each of these animals to humans. But these animals don't typically eat humans. Thus this network would be a directed network. We can link the different species of fish and other life forms that live in the ocean and their food patterns. These last two networks are examples of what is called a food-web. Other examples of networks are: electric power grids, roads, train tracks, and telephone lines.

The networks we are most concerned with in this chapter are social networks. Social networks can be defined in many ways. For instance we can think of the relationships of friends. We would let every individual be a node in the network and if two individuals are friends we would connect them with an edge. Defining what constitutes "friendship" may be more difficult than you first think. For instance a person you see everyday, trust, and have many conversations with would many times be considered a friend. But you also may have co-workers who fit into this description that you would not label as friends. In fact someone's best friend may be someone they see and interact with less frequently than many co-workers. Thus when studying social networks we generally try to put more structure on what is meant by the social relationship of interest to us. And, the structure is usually determined by the question we are interested in answering. For instance, if we are interested in the spread of an infectious disease like SARS we might define social networks based on physical proximity. If we are interested in the spread of sexually transmitted diseases we would define the social network based on sexual contact. If we are interested in trust and confiding relationships we may consider the set of people with whom you would discuss a difficult personal problem. Thus there are many ways in which we can define social networks. For the moment we will leave this problem behind and assume that you can define the social network in which you are interested and that you have access to data describing your network of interest. We now discuss how one uses some simple statistical tools to make sense of complex networks.

6.1 Network Properties

If we look at the two simple examples of networks in the figures above one can understand them fairly well with a visual inspection. However others, such as a fully defined friendship network for a large group of people or the food webs of an ocean may look to be a morass if plotted out. In this section we will discuss how to make sense of complex networks such as these using simple statistical measures and also discuss typical regularities of these measures and their implications for the spread of infectious disease. To begin I list a few important definitions:

Definition 4 The *component* to which a node belongs is the set of nodes that can be reached from it by traversing edges of the network.

Definition 5 The *geodesic path* between two nodes is the shortest path following edges of the network from one node to another.

Definition 6 The *diameter* of a network is the length of the longest geodesic path between any two nodes.

I now use these definitions in describing some key characteristics and statistical measures of networks. These characteristics will be divided up into two groups: Those that describe the entire structure of a network and those that describe individual nodes (or an individual person) in the network.

6.2 Characteristic Path Length

The first of these characteristic network statistics is the Characteristic Path Length which I will denote as L. This statistic is an aggregate statistic that tells us how close together nodes are in a network on average. One can think of L as being the expected distance between two randomly chosen nodes in a network. Specifically L is measured as the average geodesic distance between all pairs of nodes in a network. Let $D(i,j)$ be the geodesic distance between nodes i and j. Let there be N nodes in the network. One can calculate the characteristic path length as: $L = \sum_{i=1}^{N} \sum_{j=1}^{N} \frac{D(i,j)}{N(N-1)}$.

As an example consider Fig. 6.3. To calculate the characteristic path length you take all pairs of nodes in the network: $(a,b), (a,c), (a,d), (b,c), (b,d)$, and (c,d). (Because this is an undirected network I can ignore the other pairs (b, a) (c, a), etc...)

The distance between each of the nodes and node a is: $D(a,b) = 1$ because a and b are directly connected, $D(a,c) = 1$ again because a and c are directly connected, $D(a,d) = 2$ because you must go through node c to get to d. The other distances may be calculated similarly: $D(b,c) = 1$, $D(b,d) = 2$, and $D(c,d) = 1$. Note that because the example network is undirected, we do not need to calculate $D(b,a)$ because it is equal to $D(a,b)$ as is the case for every pair in an undirected network, $D(i,j) = D(j,i)$. Thus for an undirected network we only need to calculate half as many distances as there are pairs in the network, $N(N-1)/2$. Now, to find the characteristic path length, L, we take the average over all of these calculated distances: $L = (1+1+2+1+2+1)/6 = 8/6 = 4/3$. Again the

Fig. 6.3 A simple undirected network

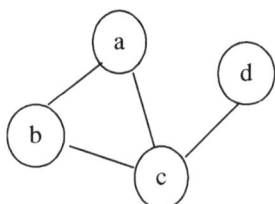

6.2 Characteristic Path Length

interpretation of L is that if you choose two random nodes in the network i and j the expected distance in this example is $L = 4/3$.

In the calculation above, we were able to calculate the distance between two nodes by looking at the network. However, many real-world networks of interest are very large and this would not be possible. For instance imagine a network of friends in a high school with 1,000 students. Further suppose that the friendship network is defined with edges between each person who considers the other to be among their 5 best friends. If we choose two random nodes in the network, and they are not directly connected, it may be hard to find the shortest path between them. Obviously it would be easy if they are directly connected, and not too hard if the geodesic distance is two or maybe even three. But, if the two nodes aren't closely connected in this network you have to consider many, many potential paths in order to find and verify the shortest one. And, you would need to do this for $1{,}000 \times 999 = 999{,}000$ pairs of nodes in the network! Obviously you wouldn't want to do so by hand! There are various algorithms that can help with the process if we load the data into a computer. But, there is another fairly direct option as well if we consider additional network representations.

Once we leave the domain of visually representing networks there are two main representations. One is called an adjacency matrix. An adjacency matrix lists each node in the network in the top row and left column of a matrix. Then as elements of the matrix one inputs a 1 as element i,j if a path exists from i to j. If a path does not exist one inputs a 0. Usually it is assumed that a path does not exist from node i to itself so that the diagonal elements of the matrix are all 0. For the network in Fig. 6.3 the resulting adjacency matrix is:

	A	B	C	D
A	0	1	1	0
B	1	0	1	0
C	1	1	0	1
D	0	0	1	0

Label this matrix as M. If a network is large, containing a large number of nodes, and sparse, most of the elements of an adjacency matrix are 0, then it is sometimes advantageous to represent the network as an adjacency list, where you list the nodes to which each node is connected. For our example network this is:

$$A\text{--}B, C$$
$$B\text{--}A, C$$
$$C\text{--}A, B, D$$
$$D\text{--}C$$

The advantage of an adjacency list is that the amount of information needed to store the network representation is much less. In our example, one needed to store 16 pieces of information in the adjacency matrix form, but only 8 pieces of information in the adjacency list form. While this may not be advantageous in our simple example, it would be important for a similarly sparse network with thousands of nodes.

Although it takes more space, the matrix representation has some nice properties for making statistical calculations. For instance, one can look directly at the adjacency matrix and determine if there exists a path of length one for two nodes i and j. In our example, this includes the following pairs of nodes: A,B; A,C; B,A; B,C; C,A; C,B; C,D; and D,C. For each of these pairs, i,j, $D(i,j) = 1$. Now multiply this matrix by itself. $M \times M =$

	A	B	C	D
A	2	1	1	1
B	1	2	1	1
C	1	1	3	0
D	1	1	0	1

Now, an interesting property of M reveals itself. The value of any element i,j of the $M \times M$ matrix is the number of paths of length two between i and j. Thus if a pair of nodes was not in our original set of distance one pairs, but our new matrix has a positive value in it, then we know that the shortest path is equal to 2. We can then make a list of all pairs of nodes that have a shortest distance of two. In our example, they are: A,D; B,D; D,A; and D,B.

For our network this is all pairs of nodes. But, if we still had pairs of nodes left, we could cross multiply this matrix by M again. The resulting values in the $M \times M \times M$ matrix would be the number of paths length three. So, we could keep cross multiplying the resulting matrix with itself until the distance between all pairs of nodes is identified. This is much easier than tracing out by hand all the possible paths that may result in the geodesic path for a given pair of nodes!

Characteristic path length has practical importance in studying properties of a network. For instance suppose you are interested in how quickly a disease will spread in a population. If the social network has a short characteristic path length then the disease may spread fairly quickly to all parts of the population. But if a population has a long characteristic path length it may take a long time for a disease to spread and the disease may even die out before it propagates across the network. Thus a social network with a long characteristic path length may be preferable if one is primarily concerned about the spread of a disease. On the other hand there may be advantages to having a short characteristic path length. For instance suppose that information about the prevention of a disease is passed by word of mouth among population members. If the characteristic path length is short it may take a short amount of time for population members to learn of the information. But if the path length is long it may take a long time to spread the information throughout the population. Other examples of cases where we may prefer a short characteristics path length in a social network are the spread of job information and the spread of a new and better technology.

6.3 Clustering

The second characteristic we will discuss is clustering.[1] At a general level, clustering measures the propensity of the connections of a given node to be connected to each other. As an example, if most of my friends also know each other, my social network has a high level of clustering. Alternatively, if most of my friends are random connections that do not know each other, then my social network has a low level of clustering.

More precisely, in an undirected graph, for any set of K nodes that are connected to a given node i there are $(K-1)K/2$ potential edges that could exist between these K nodes. (The number is $(K-1)K$ if the graph is directed.) The clustering of node i, labeled C_i, is defined as the fraction of these potential edges that exist. In a social network of friendships you may think of this as the fraction of your friends who know each other. If all of your friends know each other then your clustering would be 1. If none of your friends know each other then your clustering would be 0.

As an example again consider Fig. 6.3. Node a has two connections (it has a degree of two) in the network, b and c. Thus there is $(2-1)2/2 = 1$ potential edge between them. (The edge from b to c.) Now since an edge exists between b and c the clustering of node a is 1, $C_a = 1$. Node b also has a degree of two and thus one potential edge between its two connections. Again this edge exists, there is an edge connecting a and c. So the clustering of b is also 1, $C_b = 1$. Node c has a degree of 3 because it is connected to a, b, and d. Thus among the three connections there are $(3-1)3/2 = 3$ potential edges between them, (a,b), (a,d), and (b,d). But only one of these three potential edges exist, (a,b). Thus 1/3 of the potential edges between the connections of c actually exist. Finally, d only has one connection. Thus there are no potential edges, $(1-1)1/2 = 0$, between the connections of d. If there are no potential edges to connect among a given nodes connections, we will define that node's clustering to be 0. Thus, $C_d = 0$ in this network. We also can calculate the average clustering across the entire network by taking the average of each of the individual clustering values. We label this value as $\bar{C}$. In this example network $\bar{C} = (1 + 1 + 1/3 + 0)/4 = (7/3)/4 = 7/12$. This means that if you choose a random node from the population of nodes in this network, 7/12ths of the node's connections will be connected to each other on average. Or, if we speak in terms of friendship networks, 7/12ths of the friends of the average person in the population know each other.

Like average path length clustering also has important implications for the spread of an infectious disease across a network. Suppose that if a person is closer to many people in a population that he may be more likely to be infected with an infectious disease like influenza. Let us consider the two networks shown in Figs. 6.4 and 6.5. Both figures have a center node. The center node and all other

---

[1] See Watts and Strogatz 1998.

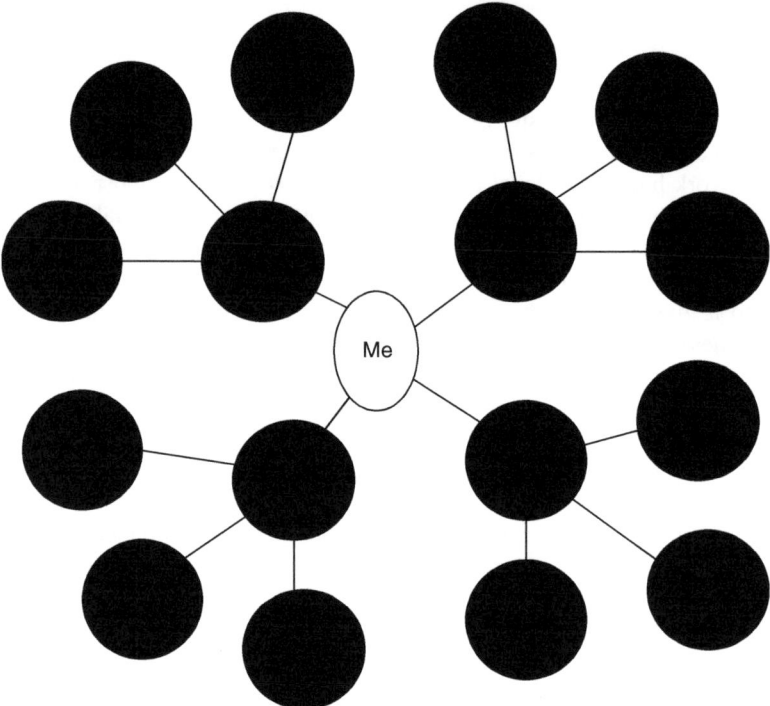

Fig. 6.4 Low clustering network

nodes in the graph all have four connections. In both cases the center node is connected to each of the four nodes immediately surrounding it. The main difference between the two networks is that the friends of the center node tend to be friends with each other in Fig. 6.5 and none of the friends of the center node are friends with each other in Fig. 6.4. Figure 6.5 has high clustering and Fig. 6.4 has low clustering. If we count the total number of friends of the center node within a distance of two we get many more friends in Fig. 6.4 than we do in Fig. 6.5. Specifically, the center node in Fig. 6.4 is connected to 16 nodes within a distance of two and the center node in Fig. 6.5 has only eight nodes within a distance of two. Thus we see a relationship between clustering and the size of a node's network within a given distance. If we decrease clustering we increase the number of nodes that are within a given distance (keeping the total number of edges constant.) Thus we see that low clustering can speed the spread of an infectious disease across a network because it can lower the characteristic path length.

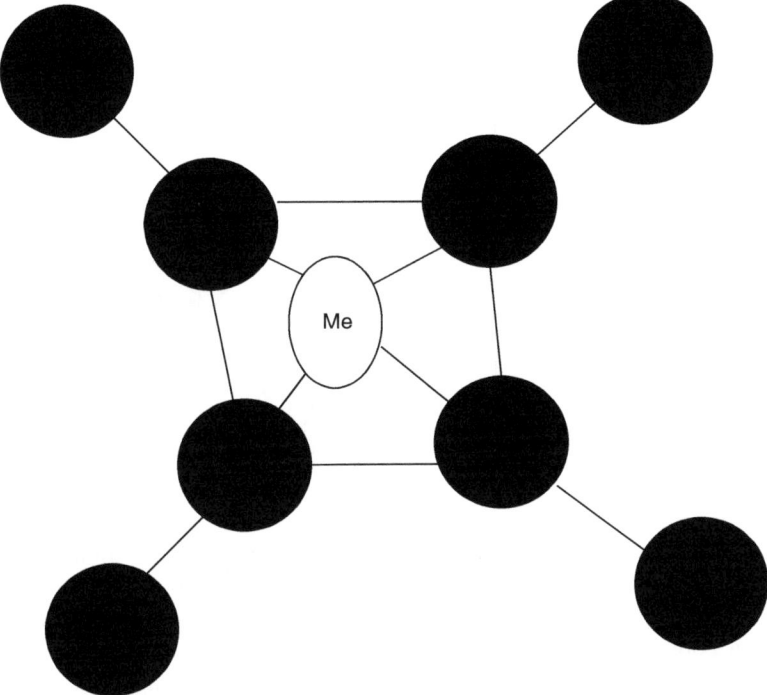

Fig. 6.5 High clustering network

6.4 Centrality

Next we consider a series of examples that each provide an idea closely related to the idea of clustering. I then use these examples to motivate the importance of our next topic, that of *centrality*. At a general level, measures of centrality try to identify the nodes of a network that are most important to its function. In the case of the spread of information on a network, nodes with high centrality are nodes that are crucial to the efficient spread of information. In the case of the spread of an infectious disease, nodes with high centrality are nodes that spread an infectious disease efficiently. And, from the perspective of public health, these high centrality nodes are also the ones we want to intervene upon (perhaps through vaccinations, quarantines or other public health interventions) in order to stop their spreading a disease.

For our first example consider Fig. 6.6. In this figure there is one central node that connects to each of the other 5 nodes in the network. But, each of the other five nodes are only connected to the node in the center. This is an example of what is sometimes referred to as a star network.

In the star network, it is clear that the node in the center of the network is most influential to the functioning of the network. If this node was removed from the

Fig. 6.6 Star network

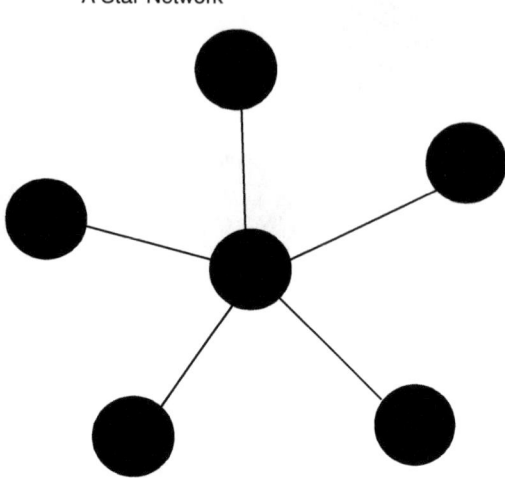

A Star Network

network, the network stops functioning because none of the other nodes are connected to each other. The network becomes a set of unconnected islands. If we are considering the spread of an infectious disease, a network of this type would present a good news/bad news situation. If any node in the network is infected, they can then infect the center node who is then able to infect all other nodes in the network. On the other hand, if we remove the center node from the disease propagation network (say through a vaccination or quarantine) then everyone in the entire network is protected from each other. We completely stop the spread of an infectious disease by removing the center node. Thus this network is very efficient at spreading an infectious disease but it is also very susceptible to falling apart.[2]

For our second example, consider Fig. 6.7. In this figure there are three groups of interest. On the left and right sides of the figure is a group of nodes that is tightly connected. Each of these groups has 5 nodes that are all connected to each other. Thus there is a very high level of clustering in each of these two groups. Then in the center of each of these groups is a single node that only has degree of two. It is connected to one node in each of the two highly clustered groups. Informally, we say that this node provides a *bridge* between the two groups.

Now consider the spread of an infectious disease. Suppose that the disease enters this population through the node on the far left of the figure. If this node is infected, all of the nodes in the left group are likely to also be infected. They may be infected by the far left node directly; or, if the far left node infects any of the other nodes in the left group, each of the other nodes in the left group will be connected to the new infections. On the other hand nodes in the group on the right side are much less likely to be infected. In fact the right side of the network can

---

[2] This is a topic that we will revisit in our next section on degree distributions.

6.4 Centrality

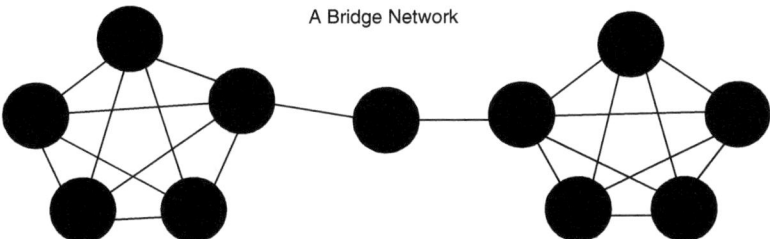

Fig. 6.7 Bridge network

only be infected if the node that serves as a bridge is infected first. And, the bridge can only be infected if the one node it is connected to in the left group is infected first. Thus one can imagine a scenario where one of the highly clustered groups have a high incidence of an infectious disease but another identical group has a very low incidence of the same disease simply because it is distant from where the infection is initially introduced into the population.

With this example in mind it becomes clear that the most important node in this example network is the node in the middle of the network that provides the bridge between the two groups. From a public health perspective, this node would provide the most important intervention opportunities. For instance if a vaccine was available, the most important node to vaccinate in this population is the bridge. If the bridge is effectively vaccinated the network is broken into two separate components. And, most importantly if one component is infected, there does not exist a path where that component can infect the other.

As an aside this concept is closely related to Ronald Burt's *structural holes*. In Burt's work a node, or person, that acts as a bridge (as in the network above) is said to fill a structural hole in the network. He argues that filling a structural hole provides a great service to information propagation in a network and may provide financial gains to the bridge. For instance maybe the node acting as a bridge connects a group of inventors to a group of investors. The role the bridge plays may lead to a new socially beneficial invention being funded, and thus provides benefits to society.

The third example contrasts with the other two because there are not any nodes that are more important than others in the network. Consider Fig. 6.8 which has a group of nodes each with degree of two. The nodes are arranged in a circle resulting in a regular pattern where the clustering coefficient for each node is equal to 0. In this network, no node is more central than any other node. If we compare this network to the star network in terms of the spread of a disease we would consider this network to be less efficient at spreading an infectious disease but also not provide many opportunities for intervention. The reason for the second point is that all nodes are identical in terms of their importance in the network. Removing any one node is equivalent to removing any other node so there are not any opportunities for strategic interventions. However, as mentioned above, this network is also unlikely to efficiently spread a disease. In order for a disease to spread

Fig. 6.8 Circle network

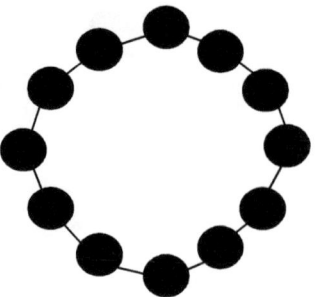

from one side of the network to another it will take many steps. If we calculate the characteristic path length of a circle network like this the average distance is the number of nodes divided by 4, N/4. (The maximum distance is N/2 and the average node is half that distance away.)

6.4.1 Measuring Centrality

We can formalize these concepts of centrality through the following measurements.

Definition 7 Degree Centrality is measured as the degree of a node.

Degree Centrality simply counts the number of edges connected to a node of interest. Recall that centrality is attempting to measure the importance of a node in a network. If a node has a large number of edges it is often important to the network structure. A star network is a good example of a network for which this is true. However as we saw in the bridge example above simply measuring the number of edges that connect to a node doesn't always do a good job of identifying importance. A second measure of centrality is called betweenness which is defined as follows.

Definition 8 Consider a network with K nodes. Let the geodesic path between two nodes, a and b, in this network be defined as G_{ab}. Let an indicator variable for node x, $E^x_{ab} = 1$ if node x exists on geodesic path G_{ab} and $E^x_{ab} = 0$ otherwise. Betweenness Centrality for node x is measured as $B_x = \frac{\sum_{a \neq b} E^x_{ab}}{K(K-1)}$.

Thus betweenness centrality measures the percentage of shortest paths between all pairs of nodes in a network that include a given node of interest. If we consider the examples above, the center node in a star network would be contained in all shortest paths in the network. Thus it would have betweenness centrality of 100 %. The periphery nodes in the network would only exist on the shortest paths to or from themselves. i.e., node x exists on the shortest path from node x to any other

6.4 Centrality

node y or from any node y to node x but x does not lie on any other shortest path in the network.

The importance of betweenness centrality for epidemiological reasons is that nodes with a high betweenness centrality lie on a number of short paths between nodes. Thus, if these highly central nodes could be vaccinated or have their behavior altered in a way that prevents them from transmitting an infectious disease then the infectious disease must take paths of greater length to infect nodes. If nodes are taken out of the shortest path the characteristic path length in the network becomes longer and infectious diseases spread less easily. As an analogy, consider flying from one small city to another small city where one makes a connection through a major hub airport like Atlanta. If for some reason you can't fly through Atlanta you may have to make three flights instead of two. It makes it harder to get from one city to another by airplane, and it makes it harder for a disease to get from one person to another because the disease must take a longer path (on average).

6.5 Degree Distribution

The third characteristic we need to consider is the degree distribution. Recall that the degree of a node is the number of edges associated with the node. If we plot the frequency of degree across the entire population of nodes in a network we get a figure showing the degree distribution. If all nodes in the distribution have the same degree, say five, we would get a spike at five and zero everywhere else. However, very few distributions have a shape such as this. Many distributions in the world tend to follow what statisticians refer to as a normal—or bell shaped—distribution where observations are fairly closely clustered around averages. As an example, the average height of a male in the United States is a little under 6 feet tall. If one were to go to the nearest large airport and record heights of men, one would expect to see some variation around this 6 foot average but not much. You may see a few people under 5 feet tall and an occasional person approaching 7 feet tall with everyone else in between. And, you would be shocked to see someone 8 feet tall! The average in a normal distribution tells us a lot about the distribution and when coupled with the variance, we know most of the important features of a distribution.

With social networks and contact networks, there tends to be much greater variation in the degree of nodes. In fact it is often the case that some nodes have a much larger degree than the average of the population. For instance consider the average web page. Most web pages you visit have only a few other pages that point to them. Thus if you think about the "average" web-page, you don't get much of a sense about how the connections on the internet work. In fact most web-pages have very few connections to them. (Think of the huge number of personal or even small business web-pages that have a very small number of other webpages linking to them, or perhaps no other web-pages linking to them.) Contrast these mostly anonymous websites with a few special web pages that have a very large number of links pointing to them. These are pages like Google, Yahoo, and Adobe Acrobat. Many, many web pages point to these web-sites. Similarly, most people have a few friends (however defined)—maybe a number low in the hundreds. But we probably all know someone who has an extraordinary number of friends—maybe in the thousands. These are the people who always know who is having a party on a college campus or who always sees someone he knows when you meet him at a restaurant. These people have many more friends than the average. Or to pick another example from social networks consider the number of sexual partners one has. Most people probably have a small number of sexual partners in a given month. But there are some individuals who have many, sex trade workers for example. If a network has a degree distribution such as this it is said to be thick tailed. All a thick tailed distribution means for our purposes is that there are always a few people that have many more connections than most. Thus if we plot a degree distribution there will be some people who have a degree in the far right of the distribution.[3]

Now, why might the degree distribution be important in analyzing social networks? Let us again consider the case of a disease; in particular let us consider a sexually transmitted disease. Suppose that there are some people in a population that have a very large number of sexual partners. Now, if a new sexually transmitted disease develops in a geographic region the person with many contacts is likely to contract the disease. And, since they have many contacts they are also likely to transmit the disease to many people. Thus having high degree nodes can have a profound impact on the dynamic processes that take place on networks.

The effect of ultra high degree nodes (sometimes referred to as "hubs") in a network provides opportunities and challenges in restricting the spread of an infectious disease. First, networks with large hubs are highly robust to the random removal of nodes. As an example consider again the network of air travel in the United States. In the U.S. there are over 15,000 airports, most of which are very small. Suppose that on a given day, 10 of these airports were not functioning (perhaps because of weather, maintenance, or some other random occurrence.) If we select these 10 airports randomly, each airport int he U.S. would have a one in 1,500 chance of being out of service. (An airport would be expected to be out of service one day in 4 years.) The chances of one of these 10 airports being a major hub like Atlanta, Chicago, Denver, etc... would be pretty small. Thus the expected effect on air travel in the country would be pretty small. On the other hand, suppose that we chose the 10 airports based on the size as measured by the number of travelers? If we shut down Atlanta, Chicago, Dallas, Chicago Los Angeles, etc... all in one day, air travel in the U.S would come to a stand still. Thus networks such as these with a very small number of high degree hubs, linking to "average" nodes

---

[3] More specifically most network structures that have been studied have degree distributions that are either exponential or scale-free. See Newman 2010, for a more complete discussion.

6.5 Degree Distribution   61

with relatively small degree (at least by comparison to the hubs) are very robust in one sense and fragile in another.

From the perspective of infectious disease, things like random vaccinations against an infectious disease like influenza may not be that effective at a macro level if our goal is to produce herd immunity. But, if we could prioritize these vaccinations by using degree or betweenness centrality the vaccinations could be much more effective. This has particular relevance for current public policy when discussing vaccine priority. Many of the deaths that occur each year from influenza are elderly citizens. The elderly population is most susceptible to the harmful effects of influenza but they are also less likely to be one of the hubs central to the spreading of an epidemic. Thus the question can be posed, can we save more lives in the elderly population by vaccinating people more likely to be hubs (people like school children) than by vaccinating the elderly directly.[4] Recently researchers have used contact data to show that, as long as the epidemic isn't too large, it can be more beneficial to the elderly to give more vaccine to the young. The decreased level of the epidemic does more to spare the elderly than it does to give them the vaccine directly.[5]

One of the problems with trying to efficiently allocate vaccines based on centrality measures is that one needs to have full knowledge of the entire network structure (recall that you need to calculate the shortest path between all pairs of nodes to calculate betweenness). One potential solution to this issue is the use of *acquaintance vaccination*.[6] With acquaintance vaccination one chooses a node at random from a network. But, you do not vaccinate the first node you choose. Instead, you then choose a second node that is connected to the first and vaccinate that second node. It turns out that this strategy is nearly as effective as choosing the most connected nodes and vaccinating them. Why does this vaccination strategy work so well? It biases the choice of node to vaccinate by the degree of a node. Intuitively, if a node has high degree it is connected to many individuals (simply by definition.) So when we choose a random contact of a random node we are strongly biasing our second selection by the degree of the second node. Nodes that have high degree are nodes that are connected to many other nodes. Thus we are likely to choose a high degree node in our second, acquaintance, selection.

6.5.1 Who Has More Friends?

Another interesting statistic that comes out of there being at least a few high degree nodes is that almost everyone has fewer friends on average than their

---

[4] Adding to the difficulty of this question is the fact that the vaccine is usually less effective for an elderly person than a young adult.

[5] See Bansal et al. 2006.

[6] See Cohen et al. 2003.

friends. As a simple example suppose that there are five people in a population. Four of them have two friends and one has four friends. Specifically, suppose that A is friends with B and C. B is friends with A and C. D is friends with E and C. And, E is friends with D and C. C is friends with all four. A, B, D, and E are all equivalent network positions. They each have two friends. One of their friends has two friends and one has 4 friends. Thus, on average, their friends have 3 friends each. On the other hand, C has four friends that each have two friends a piece. Thus her average friend has two friends. What we see here is that more people have an average friend that has more friends than she does. This is a general statistical property of networks that have a non-zero variance in their degree distribution.[7] As another example consider a distribution of class sizes at a university. Some colleges like to claim that they have a small average class size. But, when students attend they find that their average class has far more students than the average that the college reports at orientation. How can this be? Is the college lying? No it is a product of statistics. Suppose that a college has 13 classes and 100 students that each take four classes. Twelve classes have 25 students each and one large lecture class that has all 100 students. The average class size at the college is then $(12 \times 25 + 100)/13$, which is a little over 30 students. But, each student experiences an average class size of $(3 \times 25 + 100)/4$ which is a little over 43 students.[8]

The individuals in society that have above average numbers of friends are connected to more people than those who have low numbers of friends by definition. Taking this a little bit further, many of the edges in a social network will belong to individuals with many friends. Thus most of the friends that exist in a social network are individuals with above average numbers of friends. So, unless you are one of the few individuals with the most friends it is likely that your friends have more friends than you do!

This result makes for a potentially dangerous situation for accurately calculating the risk associated with acquiring an infectious disease. Suppose that the probability of being infected with a disease scales linearly with the number of friends that one has. And, suppose that you make a rational calculation to determine if you should be vaccinated for a disease or whether you should use a condom to protect yourself from a sexually transmitted disease. If you assume that each of your partners has the same number of partners that you do, you will, on average, underestimate the number of partners of your partners and therefore underestimate the risk of sexually transmitted diseases associated with unprotected sex.

---

[7] This is shown in detail in Newman 2003.

[8] Unfortunately, one can do similar calculations to find that the average time you spend in a grocery store checkout line is longer than the average checkout time in the store! It isn't bad luck, it's statistics!

6.6 Dynamic Networks

In the discussion so far in this chapter I assume that the social interactions are constant across time. Your interactions today are the same as they were yesterday and will be the same again tomorrow. In some cases this is roughly true. For instance, consider the spread of influenza during "flu season". Many (but not all) of us see the same set of family, friends, and co-workers each week throughout the time that influenza typically spreads. But, in other situations interactions change across time. For instance, in the case of sexually transmitted diseases, particularly those like HIV for which the epidemic occurs over a large time horizon, interactions are often not constant. They vary over time. Further in these cases the ordering and timing of contacts becomes important. As one example, chains of transmission now have a directional component. You may catch a disease from a partner who acquired it from another interaction at a point in time previous, but not from a partner who acquired it after your interaction.

Frequently these temporal components make analysis more difficult. But, we will demonstrate a small set of simple examples that help to demonstrate some important aspects of dynamic networks. And, we will also show how timing can help to uncover the sources of epidemics and the chains of transmission.

To begin I add a new feature to our network figures in order to account for the timing of interactions. To do so, I simply write the time periods for which an interaction occurs adjacent to the link connecting two nodes. Consider the network of interactions in Fig. 6.9. There are eight nodes in total with four of them labeled as A, B, C, and D. Nodes A and B interact in periods 1 through 5. Nodes A and C interact in periods 11 through 15. Nodes C and D interact in periods 6 through 10, and so on. Consider how an epidemic may spread in the network. Suppose for instance that node D was infected with HIV at period 0. Node D could then infect node B and node C directly. But, note that node B could not infect anyone else in the network. Node D and node B interact between periods 11 through 15 and all of node B's other interactions proceed the time in which it could be infected by node D. The case is different for node C. Node C and node D interact in periods 6 through 10. If C were to be infected it could infect node A in periods 11 through 15. But, again, the transmission would stop here as all of A's other interactions occur before A can be infected.

Compare the first network to a second network given in Fig. 6.10. There is only one difference in this network and in the first. Here the interaction between nodes B and D occurs in periods 1 through 5. Node D, the initial infected node, still has two interactions with the same two nodes but now the interaction with node B happens earlier. This is important for two reasons. The first is obvious, if node D interacts with node B earlier it provides more opportunities (in terms of time periods) for the epidemic to spread. Perhaps just as important though is the fact that node B now has concurrent interactions with three different nodes. Concurrency can be very dangerous when considering the spread of an infectious disease. If one has concurrent interactions (instead of sequential interactions) and one

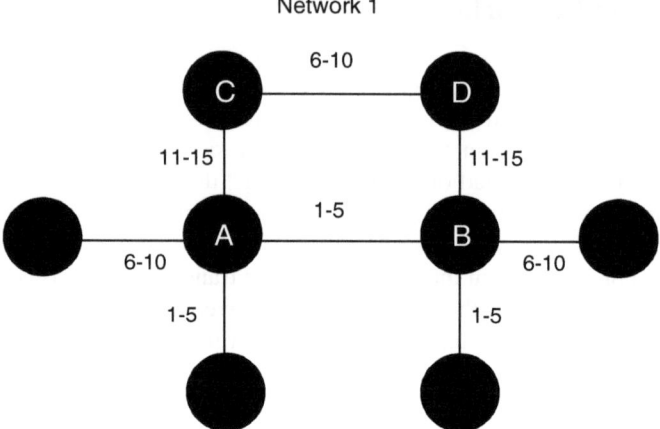

Fig. 6.9 Dynamic network 1

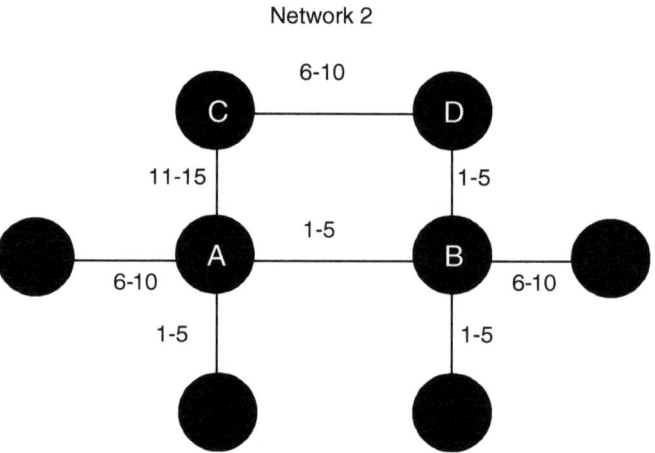

Fig. 6.10 Dynamic network 2

becomes infected, then anyone the node is in contact with can be infected. Further, if one has many interaction partners in a given period that is the period in which one is most likely to be infected. Further, once infected, the person is connected to many others to which the infectious disease can spread. This description should echo thoughts of hubs in the networks discussed in the previous sections of this chapter. In essence, concurrent interactions create inter-temporal hubs in interaction networks which are very dangerous for the spread of an infectious disease.

References

Bansal S, Pourbohloul B, Meyers LA (2006) A comparative analysis of influenza vaccination programs. PLoS Med 3(10):e387. doi:10.1371/journal.pmed.0030387

Cohen R, Havlin S, ben-Avraham D (2003) Efficient immunization strategies for computer networks and populations. Phys Rev Lett 91(24):247901

Newman MEJ (2003) Ego-centered networks and the ripple effect. Social Networks 25:83–95

Newman MEJ (2010) Networks: an introduction. Oxford University Press, New York

Watts DJ, Strogatz S (1998) Collective dynamics of 'small-world' networks. Nature 393(6684):440–442 (June 1998)

Part IV
Strategic Decision Making

Chapter 7
Strategic Public Health Interventions

In the discussion concerning network interactions above I gave several example of how to use network theory to intervene against the spread of infectious diseases. In general a policy maker would like to lengthen the characteristic path length in the network. In doing so she may intervene by vaccinating individuals with high degree or high betweenness centrality measures. In doing so it makes the structure of the interaction network less able to efficiently spread an infectious disease. There have been many studies that have looked at these types of strategies in real world populations. For instance, I, along with Phil Polgreen and Alberto Segre, look at how allocating a limited amount of vaccine by giving it first to the individuals with highest degree in the network, as opposed to randomly, greatly limits the spread of infectious disease in a hospital.[1] Others use social interaction data to investigate how different vaccination programs change the expected size of epidemics.[2]

In the remainder of this chapter I suggest that we take this process one step further by considering that individuals may change their behavior in response to either the outbreak of an epidemic or in response to an implemented policy. Essentially, I consider individuals and their responses to have a strategic element to them. First, I consider this process through the perspective of a policy maker and ask, how will the policies that I may implement change behavior and what outcomes should I expect? This will allow us to better understand effective ways to intervene and a range of things to consider when an epidemic outbreak occurs. Second, in the following chapter, I take a more sophisticated modeling strategy where I assume that individuals recognize the strategic elements at hand and behave accordingly. To do this I introduce some basic elements of game theory and provide an example where this mode of modeling is valuable for understanding the possible outcomes of public policy.

---

[1] See Polgreen et al. 2010.
[2] For example Bansal et al. 2006.

7.1 Purposeful Behavior

To begin this section I return to the idea that individuals act purposeful in the behavior. Earlier we discussed some basic tenets of economics. Primarily individuals compare the expected marginal costs and marginal benefits of decisions. If the marginal benefits are larger than the marginal costs, they take the action. In an earlier chapter we discussed how the benefit of being vaccinated declines as more individuals become vaccinated. In the next chapter I will discuss how this can play out in terms of strategic behavior among individuals. Here we discuss a situation where these marginal benefits may differ across individuals in multiple ways and how these differences may lead to different policy implications. Also note that although I will use a vaccine as a simple and straight-forward example one can think of any policy that stops someone from being infected and transferring the infection to others.

7.1.1 Varying Risk

Consider a set of individuals that all occupy a unique place in an interaction network of arbitrary but heterogenous structure. In this interaction network individuals differ along dimensions of degree and betweenness centrality. Because of these differences individuals also differ in terms of probability of infection and in terms of the marginal infections[3] that they can create in society.

In some cases this may create a dilemma for social policy. Recall that the primary objective of infectious disease social policy is to stop the secondary infections that lead to being above the epidemic threshold. In essence, you can think of a list where everyone is ranked in descending order in terms of the product of risk of infection and the marginal infections they create. The policy maker then moves down the list until this product (which is the marginal benefit of providing a vaccination) is less than the marginal cost and vaccinates everyone above this cutoff. Again note that this problem has a limit (assuming a strictly positive marginal cost) because once herd immunity is reached the marginal benefit of additional vaccinations is equal to zero.

What the individual cares about is primarily whether or not he is infected.[4] On the other hand, a policy maker is additionally concerned with the marginal infections that are created by an individual. This difference produces a tension for policy makers in some cases. As an example where the tension is especially stark,

---

[3] Recall the earlier definition of marginal infections as the additional infections that an individual creates in an epidemic outbreak.

[4] Of course individuals also care about whether family members and friends are infected but at an overall level it is not a stretch to assume that the primary concern of most individuals is the risk associated with a small subset of individuals close to them.

7.1 Purposeful Behavior

suppose that the network interaction structure is such that those who face the most risk (the ones most likely to be infected) are also the ones that create the least number of marginal infections. And, those that face the least risk of infection are the ones that create the largest number of marginal infections. In summary, suppose that the risk of infection and the marginal infections created are negatively correlated.

Now let us consider how individual decision making will compare to the socially efficient outcome. In the case described above, the individuals most likely to choose to be vaccinated (those facing the most risk) will be the ones that a policy maker cares the least about because of the few marginal infections that each vaccination prevents. In this case then, policy makers will need to provide incentives for the individuals with sufficiently high marginal infections otherwise they will not choose to be vaccinated.

As a second example suppose that risk of infection and marginal infections are positively correlated. In this instance, the risk of infection is beneficial to the policy maker. The individuals that choose to be vaccinated are also the ones that the policy maker would vaccinate if she were to choose for them. In this case the policy maker's job is easier. The priority list of the policy maker is aligned with the individual decisions that will be made. Here the policy maker's problem is simply to set the right subsidy (if necessary at all) so that enough of the most important individuals (in terms of marginal infections) get vaccinated. They need to set a subsidy to get to the correct place on the priority list but the ordering of individual decisions and the policy makers priority list agree.

Now, with these ideas in hand and combining it with our knowledge of interactions, we can consider which of the above two scenarios is more likely. Luckily for the policy makers, structure is on their side. Again, the important things that drive an epidemic are the characteristic path length (at a macro level) and the degree and betweenness (at the individual level.) Further, recalling the discussion of degree distribution above, if someone has high degree she is also likely to have high betweenness in most interaction structures. This will provide a person with both a high risk of infection and a large opportunity to infect others. Of course there are exceptions such as the bridge network example. The individual that creates the bridge has low degree and high betweenness. Thus he may be unlikely to be infected but if he is then many more people will be infected that otherwise wouldn't be. Thus the devil is in the details but on average things work in the policy maker's favor because the policy maker's actions are aligned with individual decision making.

There are other cases where policy makers are less advantaged. One of the groups that most commonly act as hubs in infectious disease interaction networks are school children. Schoolchildren come from somewhat diverse neighborhoods in a town or city, mingle together in large groups for the school day, and then return home. You can imagine your typical middle school student having six classes a day and interacting with 20 different students in each (although there is likely to be some overlap of classmates). Thus they come in contact with at least 120 people in relatively close proximity. In addition, they come in contact with many more in the hallways, lunchrooms, and other school common areas. These students then return home to come in contact with their parents and other family members (some of whom may be students in other schools with hundreds of other students). One can see that this structure provides an excellent breeding ground for the spread of infectious disease.

Because of this structure it is sometimes recommended that schools be closed in times of a serious epidemic such as occurred during the 2008–2009 H1N1 epidemic.[5] This cuts off the transmission between school children and from school children to the home. However, as has been discussed by economist Josh Epstein and others, there are dangers to this action as well. What if all of the middle school students from the previous example do not attend school but instead go to the movies or "hang out for the day" at the local mall. Or the more studious of our youngsters may go to the local library. In fact this is what was observed during recent school closures in New York City during the recent H1N1 epidemic.[6] The transmission dynamics of this scenario could be even worse than if the children attend school. Or, even if not worse, could severely limit the benefits of the school closures. Further, while many middle school children may be self-sufficient enough to be on their own for the day, other, younger children, may need to receive care. This could result in children attending their parents work place or for children to be put into other mixing situations such as day care facilities. Again, this could have very negative impacts for our efforts to control an epidemic though school closings.[7]

This is but one example to show that good intentioned policies for controlling the spread of an epidemic may have some unintended consequences that need to be accounted for. Next we talk about another such example and also provide another example of heterogeneous responses to policy.

7.1.2 Varying Risk Tolerance

Next I consider a situation where individuals respond differently to the risk of acquiring an infectious disease. To do so, I introduce the economic concept of *risk aversion*. To start, imagine you have a choice between two options. I call the options lottery one and lottery two. With lottery one you receive $50,000 with certainty. In lottery two you have a 50 % chance of winning $100,000 and a 50 % chance of winning $0. Note that the expected value of each lottery is the same. Which lottery would you pick? When faced with this question, most people pick

---

[5] For an example of research on the benefits of closing schools see, Earn et al. 2012.

[6] Flu Closings Failing to Keep Schoolchildren at Home, Bosman 2009.

[7] As another interesting item regarding this, there are large economic consequences of these school closures largely associated with parents (some of whom are needed healthcare workers) who must stay home from work to attend to their children. For estimates of these effects see, Lempel et al. 2009.

the sure thing, lottery one. When someone prefers the certainty of lottery one to the risk of lottery two, economists say that the individual exhibits *risk aversion*. If instead the individual prefers lottery two, that person exhibits *risk loving* behavior. And, if the individual is indifferent between the two lotteries, that person would be considered *risk neutral*.

Most people exhibit some amount of risk aversion. Risk aversion implies specific properties of an individual's utility function.[8] Specifically, risk aversion implies that an individual's utility function is concave. I display a utility function that is consistent with risk aversion, and a preference for lottery one over lottery two, in Fig. 7.1.

In the figure I plot utility for various amounts of money. For instance, in this example, $50,000 yields utility of 40. As the amount of money increases (decreases) the amount of utility you get increases (decreases). Relevant to the example of lottery two, $100,000 yields utility of 50 and $0 yields utility of 0. Now consider the utility value of each of the lotteries. Lottery one is easy. In that lottery you receive $50,000 with certainty, so the value of lottery one is simply the utility of $50,000: 40. Lottery two gives you a 50 % chance of receiving utility of 0 (associated with $0) and a 50 % chance of utility of 50 (associated with $100,000). One can then calculate the expected utility of lottery two as (1/2) 0 + (1/2) 50 = 25. Note that this is less than the utility of lottery one and thus this utility function is consistent with risk aversion. I display this example utility function in Fig. 7.1.

Now let us understand how this utility function yields risk averse choices. Note that the example utility function is strictly increasing but at a decreasing rate. (The rate at which it increases gets smaller.) In mathematical terms this means that $\frac{dU}{dx} > 0$ and $\frac{d^2U}{dx^2} < 0$. These are properties that define a concave function. With these properties, you can see that any weighted average of a collection of values will lie below the function. In terms of our lottery example, you will always prefer the expected value of a lottery with certainty to the lottery itself (which is consistent with risk aversion.) Also note that these properties of the utility function are consistent with the concept of diminishing marginal utility. This cornerstone of economic theory states that as you get more of something your utility per unit increases by less and less (after some point.) As an example, your 4th slice of pizza does not taste as good as your first.

One can also compare the amount of risk aversion a person displays. To understand this intuitively, consider a person with linear utility (the change in utility per unit is constant for all units of consumption.) As an example utility function with this property consider $U(x) = x$. In this case the individual would have no preference between a lottery and the expected value of that lottery with certainty. As mention above, this is the concept of a risk neutral individual. Comparing this example to the previous one you can see that the concept of risk

---

[8] A utility function is simply a function that states the amount of total utility derived from consumption choices.

Fig. 7.1 Risk averse utility example

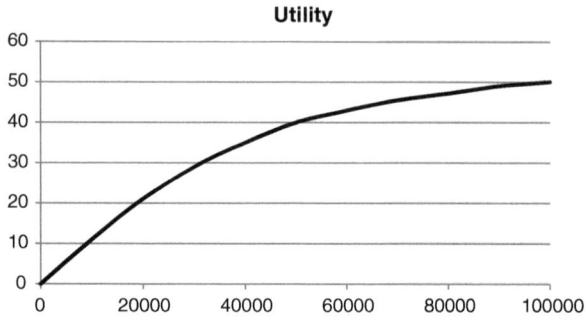

aversion is associated with the curvature of the utility function. More curvature implies that an individual is more risk averse; less curvature (closer to linear) implies that an individual is less risk averse. Thus, the utility function flattens out more quickly, all else equal, and the marginal utility decreases more quickly. As an example, consider the following two utility functions $U(x) = x^{1/2}$ and $U(x) = x^{1/3}$. The second of these functions exhibits more risk aversion than the first as can be seen in Fig. 7.2. For these utility functions marginal utility ($\frac{dU}{dx}$) would be $\frac{1}{2}x^{-1/2}$ and $\frac{1}{3}x^{-2/3}$. The utility function with more risk aversion has marginal utility that decreases more quickly than the first as shown in Fig. 7.3.

Now consider how individuals will behave when faced with the risk of acquiring an infectious disease. To keep things simple let us consider an example of sexual contacts where the probability of infection is constant per contact—twice as many contacts leads to twice the risk of infection. If we assume that individuals balance their marginal costs and marginal benefits, this will lead a more risk averse person to have fewer sexual contacts than a less risk averse person. The more risk averse person's marginal utility will drop below MC at a lower level of contacts as shown in Fig. 7.3. Specifically, for the example utility functions given above and a constant marginal cost of 0.15 the more risk averse individual will choose around three contacts while the less risk averse person will choose around 12.

Fig. 7.2 Two risk averse utility function examples

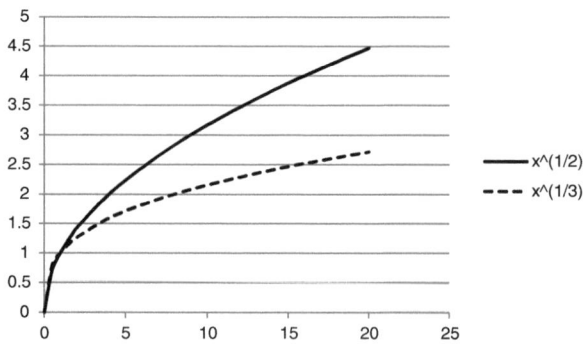

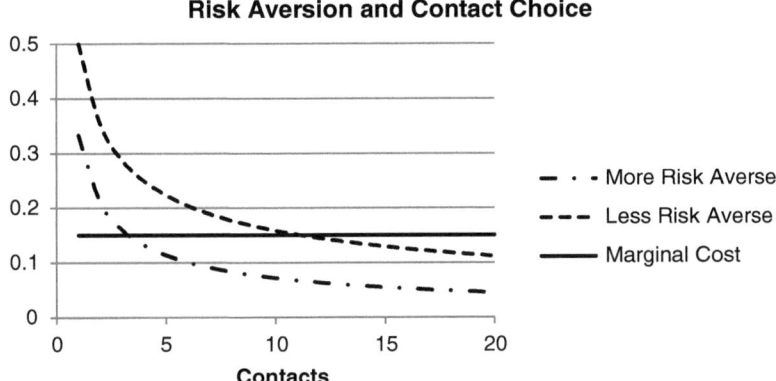

Fig. 7.3 Marginal utility and risk aversion

7.1.3 Targeted Intervention

Next suppose that a policy maker wants to intervene and reduce the number of contacts in order to reduce the spread of an infectious disease in a population where there are two groups of individuals: risk averse and non risk averse. The policy maker is going to warn the population of a new sexually transmitted disease. The population then responds to the warning in different ways. The non risk averse individual will ignore the warning and the risk averse individuals respond by lowering their contacts.

To set up a simple model suppose that risk averse people have γ_A contacts and the non risk averse group has γ_N contacts, $\gamma_N > \gamma_A$. Let us suppose that individuals pair up in a random fashion. Specifically, suppose that each non risk averse individual goes to a meeting place and pairs up with a person at random γ_N times a time period (say per year or per month.) The risk averse individuals do the same but only γ_A times per period. Let there be N_A and N_N risk averse and non risk averse individuals of each type. Specifically, there will be $N_A * \gamma_A + N_N * \gamma_N$ total contacts in the population each period. Of these, the fraction of contacts with a risk averse person is $(N_A * \gamma_A)/(N_A * \gamma_A + N_N * \gamma_N)$ and the fraction of contacts with a non risk averse person is $(N_N * \gamma_N)/(N_A * \gamma_A + N_N * \gamma_N)$. If we add a transmission rate α and an initial infected individual of each type one can then write down a simple SI type model of an infectious disease. I will further assume that the risk averse people with large numbers of contacts make up a minority of the population.[9]

As an example suppose that the following parameters specify the model: $N_N = 1{,}000$, $N_A = 10{,}000$, $\gamma_N = 10$, and $\alpha = 0.001$. I initialize the model with one infective person in each group at period 0. Now suppose that I vary the level of γ_A

---

[9] The basic set-up of this model is taken from Kremer 1998.

between 10 and 0. 10 being where there is no difference between the two groups and 0 where the policy maker has convinced the risk averse population to abstain from all contacts. (Again, I assume that the non risk averse population is not affected by the policy maker's warning.) If we set these parameters and view the fraction of the population that is infected at period 1,000 we get the fraction of the total population infected as in Table 7.1.

What is most interesting here is the non-monotonic nature of the changes in infection rates as the number of contacts decreases in the risk averse population. When $\gamma_A = 10$ and matches the non risk averse population we have very high rates of infection for each group and in total. As γ_A decreases, initially both groups have large reductions in the fraction of the population infected. But, the infections start to be more concentrated in the high risk group. Eventually, γ_A gets low enough that most of the contacts in the population are with high risk individuals and this triggers a turnaround in the infection dynamics. The high risk hubs begin interacting mostly with other high risk hubs and the fraction of those infected in this group begins to grow. Further, because of this concentration of infections in the high risk group, the fraction of the risk averse group infected also begins to climb! (Note the changes as γ_A decreases beginning with 2 to 1.0, 0.5 and 0.0.)

The example provides two lessons. First, concentrating interactions between hubs can be very dangerous for the spread of infectious disease (as was described in the chapter on interaction networks.) Second, policy makers need to be mindful of the potential for diverse reactions to policy. In this example it is possible the public warning could have harmful effects. For example suppose that the status quo had $\gamma_A = 2.0$. If the public warning dropped γ_A to 0.5 or 0.0 this would have a negative impact on the population overall. Instead it may be better for public policies to be targeted to specific populations. For instance if there was a policy that specifically targeted the high risk population it could be far more effective. Specifically, assuming $\gamma_A = 2$ lowering γ_N to 9 would significantly lower the fraction of individuals infected in all groups. But, as seen above lowering the contacts of the risk averse population at this level by one would increase the fraction infected in all population groups.

Table 7.1 Fraction of population infected

γ_A	Total	Risk averse	Non risk averse
10	0.795	0.795	0.795
6.0	0.133	0.126	0.202
5.0	0.072	0.066	0.129
4.0	0.041	0.037	0.090
3.0	0.027	0.023	0.073
2.0	0.002	0.017	0.084
1.0	0.037	0.022	0.196
0.5	0.074	0.033	0.485
0.0	0.087	0.000	0.956

References

Bansal S, Pourbohloul B, Meyers LA (2006) A comparative analysis of influenza vaccination programs. PLoS Med 3(10):e387. doi:10.1371/journal.pmed.0030387

Bosman J (2009) New York Times, 20 May 20 2009. http://www.nytimes.com/2009/05/21/nyregion/21kids.html

Earn DJD, He D, Loeb MB, Fonseca K, Lee BE, Dushoff J (2012) Effects of school closure on incidence of pandemic influenza in Alberta, Canada. Ann Inter Med 156(3):173–181 (February 2012)

Kremer M (1998) AIDS: the economic rationale for public intervention. In: Ainsworth M, Fransen L, Over M (eds) Confronting AIDS: evidence from the developing world. The European Commission and the World Bank, Brussels

Lempel H, Epstein JM, Hammond RA (2009) Economic cost and health care workforce effects of school closures in the U.S. PLOS Curr. Influenza (October 2009)

Polgreen PM, Tassier T, Pemmaraju S, Segre AM (2010) Using social networks to prioritize vaccination strategies for healthcare workers. Infect Control Hosp Epidemiol 31(9):893–900

Chapter 8
Strategic Individual Decision Making

I now move to a discussion of strategic decision making by individuals. I discuss questions such as do I choose to be vaccinated against a specific infectious disease? And, more interestingly, how does this decision depend on what other people in the population do? To answer questions like these we first need a basic introduction to game theory—the theory of strategic interactions.

8.1 A Brief Introduction to Game Theory

Game theory is the study of strategic interactions. Game theory is often used in many disciplines such as business, economics, political science, and policy modeling to name a few. Generally, a game is a situation that includes some strategic setting where outcomes to an individual depend not only on what she does but also on what some other member of society chooses. So, for instance, buying a scratch off lottery ticket and winning or losing would not constitute a game but playing poker would. In the first case, your winnings depend only on your decision to buy the ticket or not; in the second case your winnings depend on the bets and decisions you make as well as the bets and decisions that others make.

Generically, a game consists of four elements: players, rules, outcomes, and payoffs. Players are the actors and decision makers in a strategic setting. A player may be a single individual, or may be a group (ex. teams, institutions, political bodies). Rules define how the interactions occur including the timing, available decisions etc. Outcomes are the results of the decisions players make and the rules of the game; an outcome may be winning and losing or it may be some other result of the game being played. Finally outcomes are translated into a payoff. A payoff is some preference over the outcomes. In economics we usually state these payoffs in terms of utility.

There are many types of games. For now we will break games into two broad classes: simultaneous games or sequential games. In a simultaneous game players make decisions simultaneously or within the same period of time. Many athletic contests are examples of a simultaneous game. In a sequential game players take turns making decisions. Many board games like checkers or chess are examples of sequential games. Some games have a mixture of each type. As an example, in tennis, players rotate between serving and receiving, but there are many simultaneous actions and decisions that occur within each point.

For the purposes of this book we primarily discuss simultaneous games. As an example, before "flu season" each person must make a decision as to whether to be vaccinated. Although each person may make this decision at slightly different points in time, we may assume that they all make the decision before the season begins. (Of course some people may wait until influenza starts circulating and then make a decision based on the severity of the epidemic in a given year. But, we will abstract from a model of this precision for this book.)

Each player in a game must choose a strategy detailing all actions or decisions to be made in a game. More formally a *strategy* is a complete, fully contingent plan of action specifying how a game is to be played. For instance a strategy for playing the popular children's game tic-tac-toe might begin something like the following: If I move first, play middle; if my opponent follows by playing in the corner, play the opposite corner, if my opponent... etc. The important thing is that each strategy gives a detailed account of what the player will do at each and every possible stage within a game. Game theorists often refer to the *proxy test* to see if a strategy is fully specified. The proxy test works as follows: Write down what you would do at every time period in a game contingent on what has already occurred. Then give this writing to a proxy. If the proxy can take your writing and play the game exactly as you would, for every situation that could occur, then what you wrote is a strategy. If the proxy would have to ask you a question about what to do in even one circumstance, then it is not a fully contingent plan and not a strategy.

Once a strategy is defined we can begin to analyze simple simultaneous games. Suppose that there are two players involved in some interaction and that each player has two strategies available to her. Label the players 1 and 2 and the strategies x_1 and y_1 for player 1 and x_2 and y_2 for player 2. It is common to write a game of this structure in what is called the *normal form* representation as follows:

Player 2

	x_2	y_2
x_1	a, a	b, c
y_1	c, b	d, d

Player 1

Each player chooses a strategy x_i or y_i without having the knowledge of what the other player has chosen. Once the strategies are chosen an outcome of the game results and payoffs are assigned based on the numbers in the box corresponding to the outcome. We will follow the convention that the first payoff listed in a box is the payoff to player 1 and the second payoff in the box is the payoff to player 2. For instance if player one chooses strategy y_1 and player 2 chooses strategy y_2 then this results in the payoffs in the bottom right box, d, d. In this case each player receives a utility payoff of d, where d is some number. On the other hand, if player 1 chooses strategy x_1 and player 2 chooses strategy y_2 then player 1 receives a payoff of b and player 2 receives a payoff of c.

8.1 A Brief Introduction to Game Theory

A strategy is a *best response* to the strategies of her opponents if the payoff received is at least as great as she can get with any other strategy.

Definition 9 A strategy s_i, is a *best response* to the set of strategies played by all of the rivals of i, S_{-i}, if the payoff received by playing strategy s_i against S_{-i}, $\pi(s_i, S_{-i})$, is greater than or equal to the payoff received by any other strategy that could be played by agent i, s_i': $\pi(s_i, S_{-i}) \geq \pi(s_i', S_{-i})$ for all s_i' in the set of strategies available to agent i.

A common method of analyzing strategic situations such as these is to invoke the concept of a Nash equilibrium.

Definition 10 A *Nash equilibrium* in an N-player game occurs when each and every player is playing a strategy that is a best response to the strategy of every other player: $\pi(s_i, S_{-i}) \geq \pi(s_i', S_{-i})$ for all s_i' in the set of strategies available to agent i and for all i in the set of N players.

The central idea within the concept of a Nash equilibrium is that no player has an incentive to deviate from her strategy given the strategies of the other players involved. Thus, it is a rest point in the strategy space of the system.

8.1.1 Classes of 2×2 Games

One way to classify simple games is by the type of Nash equilibrium of the game. In some games each player has a dominant strategy which results in there being only one Nash equilibrium. An example of such a game is presented below.

	Player 2	
	x_2	y_2
Player 1 x_1	0, 0	1, 2
y_1	2, 1	2, 2

In this game strategy y_i is always better than strategy x_i for each player i and the resulting Nash equilibrium is y_1, y_2. Note that in this case the payoffs at the Nash equilibrium are large compared to the other possible outcomes. This is not always the case. Consider the following game:

	Player 2	
	x_2	y_2
Player 1 x_1	4, 4	1, 5
y_1	5, 1	2, 2

In this game, strategy y is always a best response for each player and, again, the resulting Nash equilibrium is y_1, y_2 with corresponding payoffs of 2, 2. But, these payoffs seem small relative to the payoffs of strategy combination x_1, x_2 which yields payoffs of 4, 4. Note that if the players attempted to coordinate on this payoff of 4, each player would have an incentive to deviate. If payer 1 chose to play x_1 player two would want to play y_2 and receive a payoff of 5 instead of playing y_1 and receiving a payoff of 4. Thus the strategic interactions in a game sometimes lead to outcomes that at first glance seem suboptimal.[1]

In other games a player may not have a dominant strategy and the best response of the player depends on the strategy of the other player. A simple game of this type is shown below:

Player 2

	x_2	y_2
x_1	1, 1	0, 0
y_1	0, 0	1, 1

Player 1

In this game each player wants to match the strategy of his opponent. If player 1 plays x_1 player 2's best response is x_2; if player 1 plays y_1, player 2's best response is y_2. Player 1 has the same incentives in his best responses so that the set of Nash equilibria is x_1, x_2 and y_1, y_2. There are two pure strategy Nash equilibria here.

There is also a "mixed strategy" Nash equilibrium of this game. A mixed strategy is a probability weighting of the possible strategies in this game. As an example mixed strategy, player 1 may choose to play strategy x_1 with a 75 % probability and strategy y_1 with a 25 % probability. If we allow players to use mixed strategies we can find another Nash equilibrium of this game. I will do so intuitively first and then show a more formal method for finding the mixed strategy Nash equilibrium.

Suppose that player 2 plays strategy x_2 with 50 % probability and strategy y_2 with 50 % probability. What is the best response of player 1? In order to answer this question we need to calculate the expected payoffs of each of the strategies available to player 1. Suppose player 1 chooses x_1. 50 % of the time player 2 will play x_2 and player 1 will receive a payoff of 1; 50 % of the time player 2 will choose y_2 and player 1 will receive a payoff of 0. Thus the expected payoff of x_1 against a 50–50 mix by player 2 is $(1/2)1 + (1/2)0 = 1/2$. A similar calculation for strategy y_1 yields an expected payoff of $1/2$ too. Thus player 1 is indifferent between strategy x_1 and strategy y_1 when player 2 chooses a 50–50 mix of x_2 and y_2. Further, if one were to calculate the expected payoff for any mixed strategy by player 1 (such as 75 % x_1, 25 % y_1 or 20 % x_1, 80 % y_1) the expected payoff would also be 1/2. By playing 50 % x_2, 50 % y_2 player 2 has made player 1 indifferent between playing any pure or mixed strategy available to him. Now suppose that player 1 chooses to mix 50–50 as well. With this mix one can do the same calculations for player 2 as were done for player 1 and find that player 2 is indifferent between any strategy (pure or mixed) that she has. So, suppose that both players mix 50–50 between their two strategies, this is a Nash equilibrium because no player has an incentive to deviate.

---

[1] For a more expansive discussion of games like these see any economics or game theory textbook discussion of "prisoner's dilemma" games.

8.1 A Brief Introduction to Game Theory

More formally, this mixed strategy Nash equilibrium has each player choosing a strategy that makes the other player indifferent between all of his available strategies. Define $E(\pi_i|s_i,s_j)$ as the expected value of the payoff to player i of playing strategy s_i against strategy s_j. A mixed strategy Nash equilibrium can be found by choosing strategy s_j such that:

$$E(\pi_i|s_i,s_j) = E(\pi_i|s'_i,s_j) \quad \text{for all} \quad s_i,s'_i.$$

In the game above define the probability of playing strategy x_2 as p, with the probability of strategy y_2 as the compliment $1-p$. Thus a value of p in $[0,1]$ defines a mixed strategy for player 2. Now start with player 1. The expected payoff of playing x_1 is given by:

$$E(\pi_1|x_1,p) = 1*p + 0*(1-p).$$

The expected value of playing y_1 is given by:

$$E(\pi_1|y_1,p) = 0*p + 1*(1-p).$$

If we set these two expectations equal to each other and solve for p this yields the level of p that makes player 1 indifferent between all available mixed and pure strategies. This value of p is the Nash equilibrium mixed strategy for player 2. It is easy to verify that $p = 1/2$ satisfies this equation. Now, do the same set of calculations for player 2 and it can be found that the Nash equilibrium mixed strategy for player 1 is also 1/2. I will use a method like this to solve for the Nash equilibrium of a strategic "vaccination game" later in this chapter.

As a final example, consider the following game:

		Player 2	
		x_2	y_2
Player 1	x_1	1,0	0,1
	y_1	0,1	1,0

At first this game may seem similar to the previous example. But upon closer inspection, one can see that there does not exist a pure strategy Nash equilibrium in this game. The payoffs imply that player 1 wants to "match" the strategy of player 2 (play x when player 2 plays x and play y when player 2 plays y). But, player 2 wants to play the opposite strategy of player 1 (play x when player 1 plays y and play y when player 1 plays x.) Thus, any combination of pure strategy choices by the players leaves someone wanting to deviate. Thus the only Nash equilibrium is in mixed strategies. Using the methods described above, one can verify that the mixed strategy Nash equilibrium has each player mixing between each available strategy equally (50 % weight on each strategy.) Finally, note that mixed strategy examples given here each resulted in Nash equilibrium mixed strategies with equal weighting on each strategy. This is not always the case. The specific Nash equilibrium mixed strategies depend on the payoffs of all available strategies. While an equal weighting resulted in a Nash equilibrium in these examples, non-equal weightings are a Nash equilibrium with other payoffs.

8.2 A Vaccination Game

I now present an example situation where game theory can be used to analyze a public health situation. As I discussed above there are multiple incentives and effects in choosing to be vaccinated for an infectious disease. One obvious one is that the vaccination offers some protection against getting infected. But remember that there is a cost to the vaccination. This cost may be a direct monetary cost. But, even if there isn't a monetary cost there is still at least a time cost to being vaccinated. If you are getting an influenza vaccine you cannot also be watching a theater performance or whatever other activity you would be doing instead of getting your shot. In addition, imagine if everyone else in the population got their influenza vaccine. There would be no need for you to be vaccinated yourself. You would be protected by herd immunity. At a more basic or realistic level, even if strictly everyone does not get vaccinated, you are more protected as more people choose to be vaccinated. And, from your perspective, because a vaccine is costly, you would rather that other people pay those monetary or time costs than you. In other words, you'd like other people to be vaccinated so that you don't have to be. Thus getting a vaccine has all of the elements of a game as described above: benefits and costs net to yield a payoff for each strategy you choose (vaccinate or not vaccinate) and those payoffs to your chosen strategy depend on what others do. If others get vaccinated your payoff to not being vaccinated grows.

To formalize this discussion consider the following game being played:

		Agent j	
		Vac	No Vac
Agent i	Vac	$-c_v$	$-c_v$
	No Vac	0	$-\pi_j \alpha c_i$

In this game I use slightly different notation than I did above. Specifically each combination of strategies yields only one payoff in a box. That payoff is the payoff to individual i. To describe this game consider a population arranged on a network where a connection between two individuals implies a contact that could lead to a transmission of an infectious disease if one of the individuals is infected and the other is susceptible. I assume that all connections are undirected. In this game each individual plays with all other individuals to whom she is connected. So, if individual i has k_i connections in the network, she plays this game k_i times—once with each of her connections. But, the agent is restricted to choose just one strategy that must be played in all of these games. Thus she cannot choose to be vaccinated against one agent and not vaccinated against another. I assume that all vaccinations are fully effective.[2] If an individual chooses to be vaccinated her payoff is the cost of the vaccination: $-c_v$. This is true whether she is matched with a vaccinated or not vaccinated connection because if she is vaccinated it does not matter what

---

[2] It is a simple extension to weight the efficacy of the vaccination with an additional parameter but this does not add to the general interest of the results that follow.

8.2 A Vaccination Game

strategy her connection chooses. If she chooses not to be vaccinated her payoff depends on the other agents to whom she is connected and to the choices of all other agents in the population (because the choices of everyone jointly determine the size of an epidemic and the probability of being infected.) For the moment suppose that individual i only has one connection, to an agent labeled j. Then the specific payoffs for each game when the individual chooses not to be vaccinated are: If individual j has chosen to be vaccinated the payoff to individual i is 0. If j is vaccinated she cannot be infected and therefore cannot infect individual i. In the other case, if individual j has not chosen to be vaccinated, she has some probability of being infective, π_j, and this infection is passed to individual i with transmission probability α. If i is infected she pays a cost of c_i. The payoff is the product of these three terms. Now, note that the probability of individual j being infective depends on the choices of all other agents in the network either directly or indirectly.

To begin the analysis I make a simplification that will be relaxed later in the chapter. Suppose that there are only two individuals i and j. We now need to find the best response of each individual. To begin, suppose that individual j is vaccinated. Then the best response of i is to choose not to be vaccinated as $0 > -c_v$. Conversely, if j does not choose to be vaccinated, the best response of i depends on the risk of infection and the costs of infection and the vaccine. Specifically, if $-c_v > -\pi_j \alpha c_i$, individual i will choose to be vaccinated. Removing the negative signs implies that i should choose to be vaccinated if $c_v < \pi_j \alpha c_i$, not be vaccinated if the inequality goes in the other direction, and is indifferent if the left and right hand sides are equal.

If we suppose this game to be symmetric (meaning there is no difference in i and j other than the labeling) we can look at the Nash equilibrium of this game. In this case, the best responses of j will follow the analysis described above for i with the labels, i and j, switched. We can then look for possible strategy combinations for a Nash equilibrium. Let us begin with a symmetric Nash equilibrium where each agent plays the same strategy. Both agents choosing to be vaccinated will never be a Nash equilibrium. Intuitively this makes sense. Like the concept of herd immunity, if everyone else you come in contact with is protected you are protected as well, even without being vaccinated. The next candidate is for both agents to choose not to be vaccinated. This would leave each player with a payoff of $-\pi_j \alpha c_i$. As we discussed above this is a best response when $c_v > \pi_j \alpha c_i$. If this inequality holds then choosing no vaccination by each player is a Nash equilibrium. What this equilibrium implies is that the cost of the vaccination is too high relative to the product of the risk of infection and the cost of the infection. In essence the danger of infection and the cost of the vaccination do not warrant the choice to be vaccinated.

Next, consider a non-symmetric Nash equilibrium where one individual chooses to be vaccinated and the other does not. Suppose that i is the individual to be vaccinated. If i is vaccinated, then not being vaccinated is a best response for j. The question then is, when is vaccinated a best response of i to j choosing not to be vaccinated? For this to be a best response, as written above, $-c_v > -\pi_j \alpha c_i$,

$c_v < \pi_j \alpha c_i$. Note that we could reverse the labels and also have a Nash equilibrium where i is not vaccinated and j is. With payoffs that fit these conditions the game becomes a coordination game where each agent choosing the opposite strategy of the other is a Nash equilibrium. As with the simple example above, when we have a coordination game of this structure there is also a mixed strategy Nash equilibrium.

The mixed strategy Nash equilibrium occurs when each individual chooses to be vaccinated with a probability that makes the other individual indifferent between her available strategies. Let the probability of individual j choosing to be vaccinated be p_j. We can now write the expected payoff to individual i of each strategy as:

$$E(Vac) = -c_v \text{ and}$$

$$E(NoVac) = 0 p_j - (1-p_j)\pi_j \alpha c_i$$

By setting these two expected payoffs equal to each other and solving for p_j we find the strategy of j that makes i indifferent: $p_j = 1 - \dfrac{c_v}{\pi_j \alpha c_i}$. Again, because payoffs are the same for each individual this is also the mix that makes individual j indifferent. So, the mixed strategy Nash equilibrium has $p_i = 1 - \dfrac{c_v}{\pi_i \alpha c_j}$ and $p_j = 1 - \dfrac{c_v}{\pi_j \alpha c_i}$.

Next I generalize this result to many individuals. Again, to keep things simple, suppose that all elements of the payoffs are identical across players. This has a hidden implication. If all of the payoff elements are the same, including π_j it must be that all individuals have the same probability of being infected. In turn this implies that the interaction network must also be symmetric or uniform across the individuals. For example, the circle network discussed in a previous chapter or a uniform random network (where each pair of agents in connected with the same independent probability.) With this assumption, we can restate the risk of infection if not vaccinated as $\pi_i = \pi_j \alpha$. I also assume that each individual has the same number of contacts and thus plays the same number of games. When we increase the number of individuals we can repeat the same analysis as above. But, I want to rule out one messy equilibrium. In the set of payoffs above that resulted in a coordination game with two players, it is somewhat easy to envision coordination actually occurring. The individuals could directly communicate on the vaccination choice and coordinate. The only issue would be that the individual not being vaccinated gets a payoff of 0 and the other individual gets a negative payoff of $-c_v$ (although this is larger than the no vaccination alternative.) Thus each individual would want to be the no vaccination individual. But, this could be resolved if the vaccine was something like a yearly flu shot. Individual i could get the shot this year and individual j next year so that the average yearly payoff is equal across the

8.2 A Vaccination Game

individuals. But, with a large number of individuals it is difficult to imagine such coordination occurring. For instance, if there were 1 million individuals in a city it would be a very difficult problem to decide who gets vaccinated and who does not in this coordinated Nash equilibrium even in the simple case where everyone is identical.[3] Thus for the remainder of this chapter I will concentrate on the symmetric Nash equilibria of the game: the no vaccination equilibrium and the mixed strategy Nash equilibrium.

The no vaccination Nash equilibrium has a simple structure even with many players; if the cost of the vaccine is too large relative to the probability of infection and the cost of infection, no one chooses to be vaccinated. The mixed strategy Nash equilibrium is a little more troublesome, but it has a nice population level interpretation. Strictly, one can think of a mixed strategy as a probability weighting on the various alternative strategies available to a player. But, with a large population, one can also think of a mixed strategy as a proportion of a population choosing various strategies. For instance, in our example vaccination game, if the Nash equilibrium implies that a player chooses to be vaccinated 25 % of the time and not to be vaccinated 75 % of the time, one can think of this as 25 % of the population chooses to be vaccinated and 75 % chooses not to be vaccinated. In addition, in the case where everyone is identical the probability of infection is also identical so that $\pi_i = \pi_j$. Now write the Nash equilibrium vaccination probability as:

$$p_i = 1 - \frac{c_v}{\pi_i c_i}. \tag{8.1}$$

Note that the comparative statics of this equation make intuitive sense. If the cost of the vaccination increases the probability of choosing to be vaccinated decreases. If the probability of being infected or the cost of an infection increases the probability of being vaccinated increases.

Now we can begin to analyze the Nash equilibrium of a simple epidemic model. Suppose that the vaccine of interest fits an SIR class of epidemic with random matching. The difficult part of finding the Nash equilibrium is calculating the risk of infection, π_i, in the Nash equilibrium mixed strategy above. The risk of infection depends on the number of vaccinations that are performed in the population as well as other parameters of the model (label these as ψ), the interaction structure of contacts (label these as Γ), and the vaccine choices of all other individuals (label this as the vector **p**). Thus one should think of the risk of infection as $\pi_i = \pi_i(\Gamma, \psi, \mathbf{p})$. The trick here is to recognize that the fraction of individuals choosing to be vaccinated in the vector **p** can also be interpreted as the

---

[3] Interestingly, diversity of individuals can sometimes help coordination in a case like this. For instance if some individuals have a higher risk of infection, they would be a natural choice to be vaccinated while low risk of infection individuals would not. Thus diversity can sometimes help with equilibrium coordination and social efficiency.

mixed strategy for the population. Denote this fraction as p'_i. This linkage is key in finding the Nash equilibrium.

With this connection we can now solve for the mixed strategy Nash equilibrium. Because a simple case is under consideration here, finding the Nash equilibrium can be done with a simple set of simulations. I can set up the simple SIR model described above as a system of difference equations, as done earlier in the book, and calculate the fraction of the population infected for various levels of vaccinations, p'_i, again interpreted as the fraction of the population vaccinated. Then for a particular set of parameter values I can calculate the level of the mixed strategy vaccination percentage, p_i, from Eq. 8.1. Noting that in equilibrium it must be the case that the individual mixed strategy vaccination probability, p_i, must be equal to the fraction of the population vaccinated, $p'_i = p_i$, we solve for the fixed point of:

$$p_i = 1 - \frac{c_v}{\pi_i(\Gamma, \psi, p_i)c_i}. \qquad (8.2)$$

I provide a set of three example below. The parameters of the example are $\alpha = 0.1$, $\gamma = 5$, and $\kappa = 0.2$ with a population of 1,000 individuals. Further assume a cost of vaccination normalized to 1.0, $c_v = 1.0$. I vary the cost of infection c_i to three levels in the example, low, medium and high. In Fig. 8.1 I show the value of p_i from Eq. 8.2 for this model over various levels of vaccinations, p'_i, shown on the vertical axis. The Nash equilibrium occurs where $p_i = p'_i$, in other words where the curve crosses the 45° line.

The solutions yield intuitive results. As the cost of infection increases the probability of vaccination (equivalently the fraction of the population vaccinated) increases. As an example, for the low cost of infection, the Nash equilibrium has vaccinations of just over 30 % of the population.

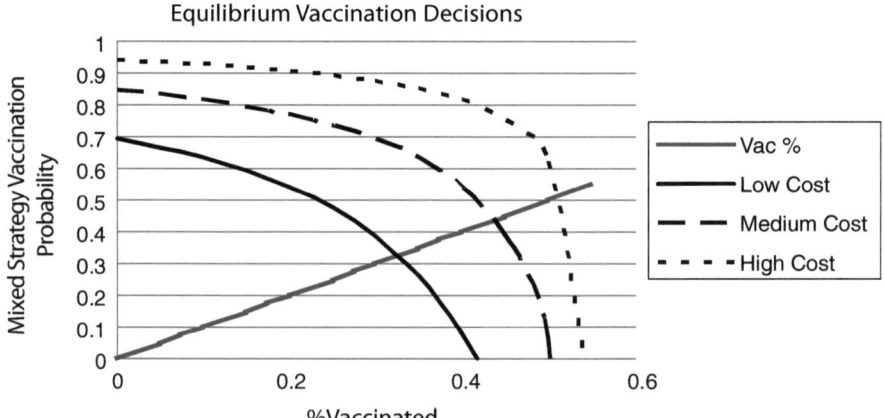

Fig. 8.1 Mixed strategy Nash equilibrium

8.2 A Vaccination Game

Models such as this can be used to try to predict the population response to vaccination programs. For instance, if one lowers the cost of being vaccinated (in monetary terms by providing a subsidy, or by providing vaccinations in a place of work to lower the time cost of receiving a vaccine) one can estimate how many more vaccinations will be taken by the population. The model above is simple. But, hopefully one can see that more advanced game theoretic models can potentially provide a fruitful path that may inform public policy in a helpful manner.

8.3 Peer Effects

One additional behavioral feature can easily be added to the above model, that of peer effects. The model above suggests that some individuals would like to free-ride on the vaccine choices of others. If you get a vaccine, I have less of an incentive to be vaccinated myself. Potentially tempering these selfish motives are peer effects. I may feel guilty or be shunned by friends and contacts if it is known that I am free riding on their costly choices. Or, for reasons of social pressure I may be more predisposed to make the same vaccination choices as my interaction partners.

Peer effects such as these can easily be incorporated into a game theoretic model in the following manner. Suppose that individual i receives a bonus to her payoff if she matches the vaccine decision of her interaction partner j. Let this bonus be τ. Now rewrite the payoff matrix for the two person game as:

		Agent j	
		Vac	No Vac
Agent i	Vac	$-c_v + \tau$	$-c_v$
	No Vac	0	$-\pi_j \alpha c_i + \tau$

I assume that the peer effects are positive, $\tau \geq 0$. Obviously if $\tau = 0$ the analysis is identical to that above. Thus I concentrate on the case where τ is strictly positive. Depending on the size of τ new Nash equilibria may occur in the game. For instance, it is easy to see that if the peer effect, τ, is larger than the cost of vaccination, c_v, then both individuals choosing to be vaccinated is now a Nash equilibrium. Each agent choosing no vaccination is also a possible equilibrium here.

I consider each possible set of Nash equilibria in the two person game in turn. I begin with the possibility of a unique pure strategy Nash equilibrium. As I mention above vaccinate, vaccinate is a Nash equilibrium if $\tau \geq c_v$. Further it will be the only Nash equilibrium if, in addition, $-c_v > -\pi_j \alpha c_i + \tau$ or $c_v + \tau < \pi_j \alpha c_i$. Thus when the cost of a vaccination is low enough, peer effects can increase the vaccination rate in the population as long as they are not large enough to create a second Nash equilibrium where both players choose to not be vaccinated.

The next unique pure strategy Nash equilibrium occurs when $-\pi_j \alpha c_i + \tau \geq -c_v$ and $\tau < c_v$. Here each player choosing not to vaccinate is a best response to either strategy of the other player. Thus both players choosing not to vaccinate is a Nash equilibrium. This is equivalent to $\tau \geq \pi_j \alpha c_i - c_v$ and $\tau < c_v$. We again see that peer effects being large enough but not too large can lead to a unique pure strategy Nash equilibrium. There are two items of note here. First, peer effects can be good in that they may create an equilibrium where everyone chooses to be vaccinated that did not previously exist. But, peer effects may also be bad in that they reinforce an equilibrium where everyone chooses not to be vaccinated. The key for policy is to attempt to encourage peer effects only when they lead to socially beneficial outcomes.

There is also the possibility of a mixed strategy Nash equilibrium with peer effects. Again write the expected payoff of each strategy for player i using p_j as the probability the other player chooses to be vaccinated:

$$E(Vac) = (-c_v + \tau)p_j - c_v(1 - p_j) \text{ and}$$
$$E(NoVac) = 0p_j + (-\pi_j \alpha c_i + \tau)(1 - p_j)$$

Setting the expectations equal and solving for p_j yields:

$$p_j = \frac{c_v - \pi_j \alpha c_i + \tau}{2\tau - \pi_j \alpha c_i}. \tag{8.3}$$

This is the probability of player j choosing to be vaccinated that makes player i indifferent between a vaccination and no vaccination. Additionally, recall that for identical player payoffs, the same equation (with reversed player subscripts) defines the probability of player i being vaccinated that makes player j indifferent. If both play with these probabilities, it is a Nash equilibrium.

The equation also helps us to defines the regions of the parameter space where each of the equilibria previously discussed exist. In order for the mixed strategy Nash equilibrium to be well defined it must be the case that $p_j \in [0, 1]$, otherwise it is not a proper probability. Now let us consider two cases where this mixed strategy Nash equilibrium may occur.

First, suppose that the numerator is positive, $c_v + \tau - \pi_j \alpha c_i > 0$. This is equivalent to $\tau - \pi_j \alpha c_i > -c_v$ which means that no vaccination is a best response to no vaccination. Further, if $\tau > c_v$ then vaccinate is a best response to vaccinate and $p_j \in (0, 1)$ because the denominator is larger than the numerator. This is the case of a coordination game with two pure strategy Nash equilibria (vaccinate, vaccinate and not vaccinate, not vaccinate) and a mixed strategy Nash equilibrium given by the equation above.

Second, suppose instead that $c_v + \tau - \pi_j \alpha c_i < 0$ which is equivalent to $\tau - \pi_j \alpha c_i < -c_v$. This means that choosing to be vaccinated is a best response to the other player not being vaccinated. Further, if $\tau < c_v$ then not being vaccinated is a best response to the other player being vaccinated. Thus there is no pure strategy Nash equilibrium and the only Nash equilibrium will be in mixed strategies.

8.3 Peer Effects

Further both the numerator and denominator of the mixed strategy equation will be negative in this case so the ratio will be positive and will be less than one because $c_v + \tau > 2\tau$. Thus again, $p_j \in (0, 1)$.

The introduction of peer effects into a simple game theoretic model can have interesting implications. In the analysis above we see that peer effects can play multiple roles from creating a sustainable equilibrium where everyone chooses to be vaccinated to reinforcing an equilibrium where no one chooses to be vaccinated as well as in between cases where mixed strategies dominate.

Chapter 9
Conclusion

My intent in writing this book was to give each reader the building blocks in three areas that are essential in confronting the spread of infectious disease. These are a basic introduction to epidemiology, an understanding of interaction networks, and a basic introduction to the economic methodologies that can help guide policy makers. I kept the models and discussions purposefully simple so that the reader could gain an understanding of basic concepts before moving on to more advanced material. As one can imagine, the more deeply one delves into the study of epidemics the more complex and complicated the topic becomes. Partly, the complexity comes from a combination of a variety of topics all interwoven into one meta topic. Epidemics spread both as a function of underlying biology and the decisions of social beings. Thus epidemiology sits at the nexus of the natural and the social sciences. In order to better understand epidemics one needs an understanding of each. I have tried to provide a basic understanding from the perspective of an economist in the previous pages.

When one looks to the future of epidemiological research it is easy to see that computational technology will be immensely helpful. As an example when one begins taking interaction networks seriously in models of epidemiology, it is almost impossible to begin to have an understanding of the spread of an infectious disease without the aid of modern computing technology. The social networks through which infectious diseases spread occur in populations of millions or billions of people (depending on your population of interest.) It is impossible to analyze or predict without using computational models in these circumstances. As such, much of the current research in epidemiology uses cutting edge computing techniques along with huge data sets to model social interactions.[1] While large data sets of social networks are being employed in these models, there remains a lack of overall sophistication in the behavioral components of these models. In essence the social science needed to build more realistic models of infectious disease still needs to be developed and incorporated into these models. Hopefully, this book may inspire someone to further pursue lines of research that will aid in this endeavor.

Reference

Epstein JM (2009) Modelling to contain pandemics. Nature 460:687 (6 August 2009)

---

[1] For instance see Epstein 2009, which discusses why computational models are needed.

MIX
Papier aus verantwortungsvollen Quellen
Paper from responsible sources
FSC® C105338

If you have any concerns about our products,
you can contact us on
ProductSafety@springernature.com

In case Publisher is established outside the EU,
the EU authorized representative is:
Springer Nature Customer Service Center GmbH
Europaplatz 3, 69115 Heidelberg, Germany

Printed by Libri Plureos GmbH
in Hamburg, Germany